LAST CALL

By Kathleen Poulton

Published by Peaceable Kingdom Inc.
79 Peaceable Kingdom Drive
Dolphin, Virginia, 23843

Last Call
Kathleen Poulton

Published by Peaceable Kingdom Inc.
Dolphin, Virginia

Library of Congress Control Number: 2015931414
Copyright © 2015 Kathleen Poulton
ISBN: 978-1-940243-67-2

Interior design and formatting by ChristianWriterHelp.com
Cover design by Kathleen Poulton

All rights reserved. No part of this book may be reproduced without written permission from the publisher or copyright holder, except in the case of brief quotations embodied in critical articles and reviews. No part of this book may be transmitted in any form or by any means—electronic, mechanical, photocopy, recording, or other—without prior written permission from the publisher or copyright holder.

Unless otherwise specified, Scripture quotations used in this book are taken from: The Holy Bible, New International Version NIV. Copyright 1973, 1978, 1984, 2011 by Biblica, Inc.

Used by permission of Zondervan. All rights reserved worldwide. WWW.ZONDERVAN.COM

Printed in the United States of America

THIS BOOK IS DEDICATED TO THE CHURCH.

ACKNOWLEDGMENTS

It was with great patience that my Heavenly Father has spurred me on to the completion of this book. I am forever grateful for his mercy. I am also eternally grateful to the Holy Spirit who has faithfully given me direction. What more can I say about Jesus? He has made all of this possible through his great display of divine love, making possible my entrance into the divine kingdom, permitting my adoption as a daughter.

I am grateful for the many people who have made a positive impact on my life through the years. In particular, I am grateful for my husband Joseph and my mother Marian. They selflessly tended to my mundane chores permitting me time for this endeavor.

CONTENTS

FOREWORD	ix
PREFACE	xi
Chapter 1: Forty Years vs. Forty Days	1
— Short Story One: "Twenty Tumultuous Years"	
Chapter 2: Deliverance from Captivity	19
— "Freedom" (a poem)	
Chapter 3: Consciousness and Consequences	29
Chapter 4: Here's Your Sign	43
— "Hurricane Isabelle" (a poem)	
Chapter 5: Fatal Attractions	51
— "The Choice" (a poem)	
Chapter 6: Humility and God's Provision	69
— Sorting Through the Sheaves	
Chapter 7: Kingdom Living	85
— Practical Application	
— Short Story Two: "Fine Dining in a War Zone"	
Chapter 8: Accepting the Call	113
— "Stand" (a poem)	
ABOUT THE AUTHOR	141

FOREWORD

Judging by the intensity of recent fearful events worldwide and the increasing display of wickedness, immorality, and evil, it is apparent that we are in the final days before Christ's return. In essence, this book is a love letter to the church. It is a call to wake up, be armed, and prepared. Many have fallen asleep and many have strayed from the path that leads to eternal life. Much of the church is powerless and perishing for lack of knowledge. This may very well be the Father's merciful last call of the final hour. Keep in mind that no one knows at what time Jesus will return for his church. By surprise, many will be caught off guard and left behind. I pray that your life will be transformed while reading this book and that you will not be left behind.

PREFACE

This book is a love letter of revelation from the Heavenly Father, opened during the end times. It is addressed to all who consider themselves a part of the church.

It is a call to realign your walk in accordance with the path that is laid out toward eternal life. The writings herein do not take any religion or social appeal into consideration as part of that directive, only the divinely inspired Word of God in practical application to daily life.

If you have repeatedly gone through hard times in your life, you will most likely find deliverance in the reading of this book.

The words are compiled in a manner that will transform your life into one of peace, power, and soundness. These words are intended for deliverance out of social pits of destruction, religious regulations, and practices that inhibit the fullness of a heavenly kingdom lifestyle.

THE LAST CALL

The beginning of the good news about Jesus the Messiah, the Son of God, as it is written in Isaiah the prophet:

"I will send my messenger ahead of you, who will prepare your way"—"a voice of one calling in the wilderness, 'Prepare the way for the Lord, make straight paths for him.'

"And so John the Baptist appeared in the wilderness, preaching a baptism of repentance for the forgiveness of sins." . . . "And this was his message: "After me comes the one more powerful than I, the straps of whose sandals I am not worthy to stoop down and untie. I baptize you with water, but he will baptize you with the Holy Spirit.""

At that time Jesus came from Nazareth in Galilee and was baptized by John in the Jordan. As Jesus was coming up out of the water, he saw heaven being torn open and the Spirit descending on him like a dove. And a voice came from heaven: "You are my Son, whom I love; with you I am well pleased."

At once the Spirit sent him out into the wilderness, and he was in the wilderness forty days, being tempted by Satan. He was with the wild animals, and angels attended him.

After John was put in prison, Jesus went into Galilee, proclaiming the good news of God. "The time has come," he said. "The kingdom of God has come near. Repent and believe the good news!"

(Mark 1:1-4; 7-15)

CHAPTER 1

FORTY YEARS VS. FORTY DAYS

"A WISE SON HEEDS HIS FATHER'S INSTRUCTION, BUT A MOCKER DOES NOT RESPOND TO REBUKES." (Proverbs 13:1)

Above all, you must understand that in the last days scoffers will come, scoffing and following their own evil desires. They will say, "Where is this 'coming' he promised? Ever since our ancestors died, everything goes on as it has since the beginning of creation." But they deliberately forget that long ago by God's word the heavens came into being and the earth was formed out of water and by water. By these waters also the world of that time was deluged and destroyed. By the same word the present heavens and earth are reserved for fire, being kept for the day of judgment and destruction of the ungodly.

But do not forget this one thing, dear friends: With the Lord a day is like a thousand years, and a thousand years are like a day. The Lord is not slow in keeping his promise, as some understand slowness. He is patient with you, not wanting anyone to perish, but everyone to come to repentance.

But the day of the Lord will come like a thief. The heavens will disappear with a roar; the elements will be destroyed by fire, and the earth and everything done in it will be laid bare.

Since everything will be destroyed in this way, what kind of people ought you to be? You ought to live holy and godly lives as you look forward to the day of God and speed its coming. That day will bring about the destruction of the heavens by fire, and the elements will melt in the heat. But in keeping with his promise we are looking forward to a new heaven and a new earth, where righteousness dwells. (2 Peter 3:3-13)

The American Heritage Dictionary defines *right* as *conforming with or conformable to justice, law or morality, and in accordance with fact, reason or truth; correct*. Also, *righteous* is defined as *the standards of what is right and just; morally right*.

We know that there are a lot of things that are not right and many do not practice righteousness. The earth is full of unrighteousness. Those of us desirous of Christ's kingdom are grieved in our spirit at the practices of the unrighteous. However, if we do not grow weary in our well doing, we will reap a harvest of righteousness that will land us an eternal home, the new heaven and new earth.

"So then, dear friends, since you are looking forward to this, make every effort to be found spotless, blameless and at peace with him. Bear in mind that our Lord's patience means salvation, just as our dear brother Paul also wrote you with the wisdom that God gave him" (2 Peter 3:14-15).

"The righteousness of the blameless makes their paths straight, but the wicked are brought down by their own wickedness. The righteousness of the upright delivers them, but the unfaithful are trapped by evil desires" (Proverbs 11:5-6).

Jesus was baptized by John, symbolizing the outward confession of inward repentance. Repentance is the necessary prerequisite for acceptance of Jesus Christ as the propitiation for our sins. This acceptance is by faith. The same Spirit that descended upon Jesus desires to descend upon you as you come up from the water. It is then that the testing begins. The outcome of that testing is where many Christians have faltered. That point of faltering or intentional disobedience to the Spirit's prompting is when their path becomes crooked and they stray from the straight path Jesus has laid before them. By taking a straight route, you will move more quickly to the destination God has mapped out for Christians on earth, which is the Promised Land, the Kingdom of God. Jesus taught us to pray for this, saying we are to pray for God's kingdom to come on earth as it is in heaven. Why do you think John said to "make straight paths for him?" If you want to walk with Jesus who walked in kingdom power to live a victorious life, you will get there much faster if you walk in obedience.

The reason it took so long for the Israelites to enter the Promised Land was their disobedience. Had they prepared a straight path for themselves, they would have arrived thirty-nine years earlier—that's half a lifetime. It takes most of us at least that long to enter into the promised land of kingdom power, peace, abundant provision, and rest. I know that you would like to be living in the promised kingdom, and you can be. Read on to find out how.

Peter said: "Dear friends, I urge you, as foreigners and exiles, to abstain from sinful desires, which war against your soul" (1 Peter 2:11). I would like to expound on "trapped by evil desires" (Proverbs 11:5-6). First, let's look at the word *trapped*. *A trap is a stratagem or device employed to betray, trick, or expose an unsuspecting victim. A stratagem is a military maneuver designed to deceive or surprise, a device employed is simply the means by whatever or whoever is working to betray, trick, or expose you.* Second, let's look at evil desires. *Evil* means *morally wrong; wicked, causing ruin, injury, and pain*. Evil desires are harmful. They can be characterized by anger or spite and are indicative of future misfortune or destruction when put into action. *Desire is a wish, longing, or craving*. I pull this all together in the following story, an analogy using the unfaithful behavior and disobedience of two believers which causes a major detour off the straight path.

Twenty Tumultuous Years

These years were marked by haste, confusion, disorder, and irregularity. A couple married for over thirteen years goes through a time of testing and it ends in near disaster.

A couple met. He was a prodigal Christian. She was an alienated Catholic, searching for the truth, who wanted to accomplish some great feat of humanitarianism. They met and he offered to help her. They moved to a new area to start a project she had dreamed of ever since she was a young girl, to feed and shelter all starving and unwanted animals and children. She came up with a plan: Open an animal sanctuary to provide a home for abused and orphaned animals, and reach out to people through the animal project.

The man had gotten into some trouble before the two met, which caused him to become accountable to a probation officer. After moving with her to a new state, he became accountable to a new probation officer. She went with him to the first visit with the new probation officer. At that meeting the probation officer told him that it was actually illegal to live together in that state, and it would not look too good for him to do anything illegal, given his probation. So after they left that meeting, the man asked the woman to marry him. She agreed and the two got married.

A short time after they were married, her husband gave her a book to read. Though she had read similar books before, this one sparked her interest in reading the Bible. In turn, this set her on the path leading to becoming a born again Christian. One night she had a dream in which she saw hell. What she saw was so awful that she couldn't even remember it all—all she knew was that she saw hell and did not want to go there.

She made some radical changes in her lifestyle. The couple found a Pentecostal church to attend. They were taken very much by the teaching there. The man assisted in constructing a new building for the church. After the building was completed they began attending a different church that was closer to their home, a more radical fellowship. The man helped their new church construct a new building. The couple became close with the pastor and leadership team and the woman got involved in ministry with them.

When great controversy and opposition developed over the couple's animal sanctuary, in an effort to pursue peace, the couple moved to an area where they could afford to purchase a larger tract of land for the project. Unfortunately, the move alienated the couple from their new church.

Shortly after their move, due to a tragic incident at the church, the pastor and his wife and one of the couples with which they were closest relocated to another state. Due to the distance, they eventually lost contact with the pastor, his wife, and their closest Christian friends. They were left with no Christian friends and no church to attend nearby. They purchased a large tent and began to hold Bible studies on Sunday mornings, inviting the few new people they met. Unfortunately, one day the tent was destroyed by wind, leaving them no place to meet.

After some searching, they started to attend a struggling nondenominational church. She began to teach adult Sunday school classes and wrote a play for the youth of the church. Shortly after they parted with the church, it dissolved. They then found a very small nondenominational church and began to attend. It was not at all like the Pentecostal churches to which they had grown accustomed over their short time as committed Christians. Though the man was bored with the church, his wife started a small children's ministry at the church and the animal sanctuary.

The Lord was truly blessing the couple all the while. They started a construction business that became very prosperous. She bought another farm as a business investment, to grow alfalfa. The animal sanctuary project turned out to be a lot of hard work. Though she was dedicated to it, her husband was given to play more than work. He was led astray by his own desires which landed the couple in a divorce. He was guilty. She felt hurt, abandoned, confused, and angry. He went on to live with the woman with whom he had been partying and having an affair. She was in her mid-thirties and devastated.

After giving him the construction business they had started, she had to start over again and find work. She was left to support over 200 animals and maintain the farms, all alone. She could not afford to maintain both farms and soon had to give up one of them. She picked back up some old habits, stopped the children's ministries she had started, and went to work full time. She started dating a game warden with whom she had business dealings related to the animal project. This warden had started hanging around the project even before she and her husband separated, but more frequently after their separation. Her relationship with him did not last long.

Filling the Void

After trying several jobs, and being pretty beat up by the community, she went on to establish her own business which was quite prosperous. After many years of hard work, she opened up her nonprofit animal sanctuary to the public. Due to her workload, she was in and out of church, though mostly out. The "divide and conquer" design almost worked again in her life (as you will hear later in this story).

Her husband went on with his life of adventure. He had a good time partying with his new lover for the first few years. He gave up his construction license and the business and just worked wherever word of mouth led him, eventually building log homes for another contractor. He became an avid hunter in the winter and did a lot of scuba diving in the summer. When the real void hit him, he filled it with hunting, sports, games, and anything entertaining. One of the favorite toys he had acquired was his quite expensive gun collection. He finally grew tired of his party lifestyle and left his lover of thirteen years. She kept his expensive gun collection, his carpentry tools, and everything else that was important to him. He left with only a few clothes and what he could fit in his truck.

Deepened Deception

Just before he left her, he found out that she and the same game warden that had briefly dated his ex-wife had a bet that they could split up he and his wife. For thirteen years, they thought they had won. This was an obvious design Satan had set on the couple that went unnoticed for all those years.

On her part, the ex-wife dated several men, spending over seven years dating a mutual friend of her and her husband. This relationship developed only because neither could find a suitable partner to date, though they had both been searching in all the wrong places. They went out together all the time, each hoping to meet someone, while pretty much living together. She finally decided she had to break it off, knowing she loved him only as a dear friend. At forty-five, she was getting anxious. She had no children and was tired of being taken advantage of, tired of working all the time, and very lonely.

Finally, she thought she had found an end to her anxiety. An old neighbor of her and her ex-husband, a divorcee with whom she rarely had contact, came back into the picture and swept her off her feet. After dating him only two months, she married him. Not long after the marriage, she knew she had made a mistake. It turned to be a near fatal disaster, and ended in divorce. During this disaster she had started to attend an Evangelical church and was starting to rely on God again.

Turning Around

At this point in her life, she was broken, deeply hurt again, devastated, and had to start over. She was at rock bottom. She moved back home to her farm. During this time she made her mind up to give her life totally over to the Lord's hand and his work. She spent nearly two years just studying the Bible and teaching it on her own to seniors at a local senior center and inmates at a jail where she worked. She worked both of these jobs part time and most weekends. Whenever she was off, she attended a Pentecostal church and in it found a holy assembly place to worship, led by a pastor whose teaching was powerful and Bible-based.

One day, while she prayed and forgave people who had recently hurt her, her long lost ex-husband came to mind. She had never forgiven him, but knew she had to. She did not know where he was, so she left a message with his mother that she wanted to speak with him. He would later tell her that when his mother mentioned her name and that she wanted to speak to him, his spirit leaped inside him. He called and she forgave him. When he came to visit her, as soon as she saw his face, she knew that she had never stopped loving him—she just hated what he had done.

A Second Chance

The two were remarried. Even though he lost his job shortly after they were reunited and brought back years of unpaid bills, blessings still poured into their lives. She landed a very good job working for a subcontractor, making the most money she had ever made in her life. She once again became very dedicated to working at that job, doing her work as if working for the Lord.

The job became very stressful. Her first boss was demanding and put a heavy workload on her, causing her to work long hours, seven days a week. Whenever he was in town, he was flirtatious, demanding of her time, and tried her with attempted "extracurricular activities." She became a Christian witness to him and they became good friends.

The client they worked for was unreasonable, demanding, intimidating, and never seemed satisfied, no matter how hard she or her boss tried. This created a very stressful working environment. She was compliant, submissive, and accommodating to all of the demands as she felt the Lord would have her to be. The company decided to remove her boss due to complaints from the client.

Her next boss was extremely intimidating, threatening, and said she was making way too much money. He put her on a salary and took away her overtime pay. Once again, she remained submissive to an abusive boss, doing all he asked, working harder and harder for less money. She persevered in her submission, trying to be a Christian witness to him and the two of them ended up getting along very well.

A month short of her working for the company for two years, her boss came in one day to say the company was going a different direction that she was not part of the plan, and she had to go. He had tears in his eyes and said that he wanted her to know this was not his doing. Needless to say, he came in like a lion and went out like a lamb.

She did not understand why she was let go from her job, especially after she had bent over backwards to try to make the operation a success. She had gone above and beyond what the company expected of her and jumped through all the hoops the client put up. In fact, the long hours and stressful working environment had taken quite a toll on her physically, not allowing much time for rest.

One thing she did know is that she trusted her Heavenly Father and that he had another plan for her life. She was heartbroken over the way she was treated. She felt used and unappreciated by her superiors, the client, and especially the many people she had hired and tried to help who deserted her. Yet she knew she could not be bitter or retaliate.

Redirection

Her Heavenly Father had prepared her for the transition. She was let go on a Wednesday. While at church the Sunday before, a member of the worship team with whom she had rarely conversed came up to her and said, "God said that his anointing is on you, and I was wondering if I could pray for you." Of course she said okay. So the worship team member prayed that God would place her where he wanted her to be, and that she would find that place. She agreed. She knew this was for real. She had recently enrolled in a ministry program her church offered. The program allowed her to be credentialed through the denomination. She was able to do this and still work, but had put the things she knew God wanted her to do on the back burner due to her job.

That following Monday, a flock of seagulls showed up on her farm. Now this was something she had never seen in the twenty-four years she lived there—it was unnatural. The farm was not near any body of water seagulls would frequent. The seagulls had a very special meaning to her and she was greatly encouraged at the sight of them, knowing that it meant something, and that God was speaking through their appearing.

Her husband came out to see the seagulls. They circled around her several times and then went to land in the field. One of the birds came back and circled around her. She heard it say, "Come on, it's time to go! Come with us." She then heard the Lord say, "As many as are the birds you see are the places you will carry my words." She stood there in amazement for about fifteen minutes. Then she headed off to work, pondering the experience all day. Two days later, she lost her job without warning and for no apparent reason.

Her health insurance was about to run out, so she decided to go to the doctor for a routine checkup. He found a huge tumor. Within a week, she was in the hospital to have it removed. She went from going full speed to no speed as she lay in the hospital. She acquired an infection from the surgery that put her at death's door. It kept her in the hospital an extra week. An experience like this will cause one to quickly evaluate one's life and priorities, and it was no different for her. What if she died and faced her Lord and had to give an account? Had she done all he had asked her to do? She knew that God had a call on her life that she had not wholeheartedly pursued. She did not want to waste any more time on her interests or her career; it was going to be God's way all the way from then on.

Exposing the Snare

After a few months of lying in bed recovering, at the mercy of others to assist her with basic needs, she became very humbled. "Lord, where did this come from?" she prayed. "A root of bitterness," she heard in reply. That tumor had not gotten that big overnight. It had taken her a long time to forgive her husband. She also knew she had yet to forgive many people who had recently hurt her. Though she had gone out of her way to help them, they made slanderous accusations and spread gossip and lies about her. She then realized what had happened. The following scriptures came to her mind: "In your anger do not sin": Do not let the sun go down while you are still angry, and do not give the devil a foothold" (Ephesians 4:26-27), and "Anyone who has been stealing must steal no longer, but must work, doing something useful with their own hands, that they may have something to share with those in need" (Ephesians 4:28). Is anger in the same category as stealing? Yes it is! Our Heavenly Father tells us what not to do and how to act for our own good. Anger can cause you to sin. What a trap!

Her husband had been taken for almost everything he had due to the company he kept and the choices he made. He returned to his wife with practically nothing but a guilty conscience. She forgave him, but was bitter over the time lost and that while he played he had not paid his bills. She had been stuck with taking care of business the entire time they were separated. She was resentful over the time she had spent working all those years to try to maintain the farm while he played.

All this had worked as a fertilizer on the tumor. Unforgiveness was the seed of the growth that developed within her, fed by resentment and bitterness. If she was to forgive him, it must be total and at a cost to her, just as it cost Jesus when he gave his life for her. When she forgave, she was healed.

Set Free

Most of us would ask, what did this woman do that was so bad that she deserved all of this abusive treatment? Absolutely nothing! What did Jesus do to deserve the way that he was treated? Absolutely nothing! Not that I am comparing this woman to Jesus, but anyone who truly follows Jesus must take his or her cross and follow him. At times, we are called to make a sacrifice on our behalf for the well-being of others.

We are also called to overcome emotionally destructive snares, even those like the woman in the story had endured that were orchestrated to deceive and emotionally betray her. These circumstances were designed to tempt her to fall prey to the development of a root of bitterness. (Recall that evil can be characterized by anger and indicate future misfortune or destruction.) The woman had been very angry with and bitter toward her husband for many years. In harboring these emotions, she eventually experienced the destructive effects in her own physical body.

In Hebrews 12:15, we read, "See to it that no one falls short of the grace of God and that no bitter root grows up to cause trouble and defile many." I have read that emotions like bitterness, resentment, and unforgiveness can actually prevent the body from releasing toxic material that can lead to disease. Stress also is an inhibitor of healing. It is no wonder that our Lord said, "my people are destroyed from lack of knowledge" (Hosea 4:6).

The good side to this story is that in God's great mercy, and as a faithful Father, he allowed for the guilt-stricken husband to be forgiven and his relationship with his former wife to be restored in a second marriage. God in his mercy, allowed the wife who repented and forgave to be healed of the tumor that had grown within her for years due to a root of bitterness within her, stemming from anger as a result of her hurt and unforgiveness. God led her from an intensely stressful lifestyle to a heavenly kingdom; one of abundant provision, peace, healing, and rest. She now had God's work and plan for her life set in order as her first priority. God gave her a second chance at life to honor him, serve him, and accomplish his will for her life—and to do so side by side with the husband she always loved. Our Heavenly Father knows what is best for us even though, at the time, we may not see our circumstances that way.

After reading this short story, we can make many applications to "trapped by evil desires." We can learn the following lessons and more from this story:

1. Satan comes to rob, steal, and destroy.
2. Satan will tempt you.
3. There is a real spiritual battle going on.
4. Sometimes people do not know which spirit is influencing them.
5. Bad company corrupts good character.
6. You will be tested.
7. Forgiveness is a choice.
8. You reap what you sow
9. Our plans are not always in line with God's.
10. As a Christian, you will be hated and persecuted without cause.
11. Do not let the sun go down on your anger and do not give the devil a foothold.
12. Harboring ill emotions can make you physically ill.
13. Living your life according to God's Word will cause you to be a witness.
14. Forgiveness brings healing.
15. It is never too late to repent.
16. God is a God of second chances.

17. God is in the restoration business.
18. God's ways are higher than our ways.
19. God is faithful even when we are not.
20. God never leaves or forsakes you.
21. God works all things together for the good of those who love him, who are called according to his purpose.
22. God heals us.
23. God provides for all our needs.

Here are some thoughts, after reading the story:

"Stern discipline awaits anyone who leaves the path; the one who hates correction will die" (Proverbs 15:10). When we go through times of testing, Satan would like to take control of our soul (thoughts and emotions), so he will set designs on us to try to trick and trap us into a thought pattern that is contrary to the Word of God. Testing is totally different from tempting. Read the book of Job for a good example. Satan also would like to stop you from fulfilling your God-given destiny. Just remember that he cannot stop what God plans to do for you or through you.

We are created with a free will. You can make the path as straight as you want to. You can choose to take detours around obstacles and obstructions, as Jesus said you can speak to them and they will be removed. We spend a lot of time walking up and down and around mountains and hanging out in valleys. We choose to forgive; it does not come naturally. Through your choices you may be detained in carrying out God's will for your life, but if you ask for the Lord to help you, He will do so and also turn everything for your good!

As Elihu said in the book of Job, "For God does speak—now one way, now another—though no one perceives it" (Job 33:14). Oftentimes we pray for a way out of certain circumstances we find ourselves in when we should be praying and asking why we are in the circumstances. In my life, asking why in prayer has worked to my benefit.

It was when I repented that circumstances changed. It was when I changed my mind-set that I was healed.

What appears to be God's apparent harshness in chastening human beings, as depicted in the book of Job, Elihu saw in reality as an act of love. For in this life, we are never punished in keeping with what we fully deserve. When Job repented, he was fully restored.

Just as Christ's resurrection followed death, so the believer who dies with Christ is raised to a new quality of life, here and now. Jesus said, "But seek first his kingdom and his righteousness, and all these things will be given to you as well" (Matthew 6:33).

Worldly Possessions vs. Spiritual Possessions

> And he said: "The Son of Man must suffer many things and be rejected by the elders, chief priests and teachers of the law, and he must be killed and on the third day be raised to life."
>
> Then he said to them all: "Whoever wants to be my disciple must deny themselves and take up their cross daily and follow me. For whoever wants to save their life will lose it, but whoever loses their life for me will save it. What good is it for someone to gain the whole world, and yet lose or forfeit their very self? Whoever is ashamed of me and my words, the Son of Man will be ashamed of them when he comes in his glory and in the glory of the Father and of the holy angels." (Luke 9:22-26)

We have a tendency to think of possessions from a material aspect only. The woman in the story you read earlier in this chapter ("Twenty Tumultuous Years") had to deny and give up some prideful emotions to follow Jesus in a walk of love. What a blessed ending to that story. How different the story would have ended if the woman had not heeded God's call to forgive and sacrifice her pride.

"So, as the Holy Spirit says, "Today if you hear his voice, do not harden your hearts as you did in the rebellion, during the time of testing in the wilderness, where your ancestors tested and tried me, though for forty years they saw what I did. That is why I was angry with that generation; I said, 'Their hearts are always going astray, and they have not known my ways.' So I declared on oath in my anger, 'They shall never enter my rest'" (Hebrews 3:7-11).

Is there something in your life that comes to mind that you are not satisfied with and complaining about rather than giving thanks to God for his provision? Do you trust God's Word and his truth? Do you apply it in all areas and aspects of your emotions and life? Do you refrain from pushing it aside and saying, "My life was easier before I was a Christian"? Do you feel that you have been treated unfairly and unjustly? Do you feel that you have been shortchanged in life? Do you wish you had something you do not have or that you were not in a situation you are in? Are you reacting the way you are because of how you have been treated? Are you thinking, *I am the way I am and reacted in the manner I did because of this situation in my life, because someone did _____ to me and they are wrong*? Putting all aside, walking with Jesus requires accountability through and through, inside as well as outside. When we make the application of God's words and ways in our lives, regardless of how other people act, we find peace, rest, and freedom from that which inhibits us from walking a kingdom lifestyle.

"See to it, brothers and sisters, that none of you has a sinful, unbelieving heart that turns away from the living God. But encourage one another daily, as long as it is called "Today," so that none of you may be hardened by sin's deceitfulness. We have come to share in Christ if indeed we hold our original conviction firmly to the very end. As just been said: "Today, if you hear his voice, do not harden your hearts as you did in the rebellion" (Hebrews 3:12-15).

Does something come to mind that you are doing and need not be? Are you rebellious to God's direction? Have you developed a mind-set or given in to emotions that are contrary to wholesome living and God's Word and directions for dealing with others? Have you become impatient with your situation and do you take matters into your own hands, compromising what you know to be right, only to make a mess of your life? Are you murmuring, grumbling, and complaining? If you answered yes to any of these questions, repent and ask God to help you and he will. Then you can start on the straight path to a kingdom lifestyle, today.

CHAPTER 2

DELIVERANCE FROM CAPTIVITY

Referencing stories of the Old Testament, the writer of Hebrews makes a resounding point: "Who were they who heard and rebelled? Were they not all those Moses led out of Egypt? And with whom was he angry for forty years? Was it not with those who sinned, whose bodies perished in the wilderness? And to whom did God swear that they would never enter his rest if not to those who disobeyed? So we see that they were not able to enter, because of their unbelief" (Hebrews 3:16-19). If we are obedient, trust and believe God, and take him for his Word, we will enter his rest.

Just as Moses led the Israelites out of bondage to slavery in Egypt, God led us out of slavery to sin through Jesus Christ. Like the Israelites, we can find ourselves grumbling and complaining about the provision God has miraculously made for us. We were miraculously delivered from captivity to sin by Jesus Christ. Why would we not want to persevere in our well doing? Why would we want to go back to a life of bondage to sin? What do you believe God's Word about? All of it is applicable to us—all of it—no buts about it. "For the word of God is alive and active. Sharper than any double-edged sword, it penetrates even to dividing soul and spirit, joints and marrow; it judges the thoughts and attitudes of the heart. Nothing in all creation is hidden from God's sight. Everything is uncovered and laid bare before the eyes of him to whom we must give account" (Hebrews 4:12-13).

In reading these passages, I can see where Satan finds the background to set up his failure design on people. The thought patterns and attitudes of the heart are war zones. Without the double-edged sword, even the protection of joints and marrow are open to attack. Many times, cures for diseases can be found in God's Word. Just think about the word *disease*: *dis, meaning the absence of*, and *ease, meaning the condition of being without discomfort, pain or worry*. Now you can totally understand why Jesus said to take upon yourself his yoke to find rest for your soul, and that he is gentle and humble. He said: "Come to me, all you who are weary and burdened, and I will give you rest. Take my yoke upon you and learn from me, for I am gentle and humble in heart, and you will find rest for your souls. For my yoke is easy and my burden is light" (Matthew 11:29-30).

> Therefore, since the promise of entering his rest still stands, let us be careful that none of you be found to have fallen short of it. For we also have had the good news proclaimed to us, just as they did; but the message they heard was of no value to them, because they did not share the faith of those who obeyed. Now we who have believed enter that rest, just as God has said, "So I declared on oath in my anger, 'They shall never enter my rest.'" And yet his work has been finished since the creation of the world. For somewhere he has spoken about the seventh day in these words: "On the seventh day God rested from all his works." And again in the passage above he says, "They shall never enter my rest." Therefore since it still remains for some to enter that rest, and since those who formerly had the good news proclaimed to them did not go in because of their disobedience, God again set a certain day, calling it "Today." This he did when a long time later he spoke through David, as in the passage already quoted: "Today, if you hear his voice, do

not harden your hearts." For if Joshua had given them rest, God would not have spoken later about another day. There remains, then, a Sabbath-rest for the people of God; for anyone who enters God's rest also rests from their works, just as God did from his. Let us, therefore, make every effort to enter that rest, so that no one will perish by following their example of disobedience." (Hebrews 4:1-11)

Have you heard God's Word and chosen to ignore it or not put it into practice? Is your life stressful? If it is, it might be time for an evaluation of your priorities. Oftentimes the stress that we undergo is self-inflicted. Is what you're doing really worth the price you are paying for it? Rest is a peaceful situation, free from external threat and oppression, and untroubled within by conflict.

"For this reason Christ is the mediator of a new covenant, that those who are called may receive the promised eternal inheritance—now that he has died as a ransom to set them free from the sins committed under the first covenant" (Hebrews 9:15).

"But to each one of us grace has been given as Christ apportioned it. This is why it says: "When he ascended on high, he took many captives and gave gifts to his people"" (Ephesians 4:7-8). Jesus told us to take on his yoke and he would give us rest, and to commit our way and plans to the Lord and we would be successful. Moses led them out of Egypt; out of slavery. Jesus led us out of captivity to the slavery of sin.

When I think of the Israelites, how God loved them so much, and how he commissioned Moses to lead their deliverance out of slavery, I thought about what Jesus did for me.

FREEDOM

My chains are gone, I have been set free
This promise is for you as well as me
So pray to God that you will see

What inhibits you from being free.
If you are bound by sin
Let repentance begin
Let God's Word become your guard
To keep your heart from becoming hard.
Today is the day to walk in God's way
And in your heart, keep his words to stay
To keep you from harm
And all alarm.
For peace and for rest
Then your life as a witness will be the best
You will be all you have been enabled to be
Sharing your life for others to be set free.
(Kathleen Poulton, October 8, 2014)

To apply the Word of God to your heart and life, you need to know it. How do you come to know it? You read and study it. This is a life or death question: Are you ready to stand before God and give an account of your actions?

Trials and Temptation

"Therefore, since we have a great high priest who has ascended into heaven, Jesus the Son of God, let us hold firmly to the faith we profess. For we do not have a high priest who is unable to empathize with our weaknesses, but we have one who has been tempted in every way, just as we are—yet he did not sin. Let us then approach God's throne of grace with confidence, so that we may receive mercy and find grace to help us in our time of need" (Hebrews 4:14-16).

Let our daily prayer and petition be asking the Holy Spirit to reveal what is in our hearts so that we may repent and receive God's grace and mercy to help us through all we do, that he would cause us to be victorious and successful. "But who can discern their own errors? Forgive my hidden faults. Keep your servant also from willful sins;

may they not rule over me. Then I will be blameless, innocent of great transgression" (Psalm 19:12-13).

"There is a way that appears to be right, but in the end it leads to death" (Proverbs 14:12). Is life a struggle for you? Are you working hard and tired all the time? Could it be you are carrying a yoke not placed on you by God, but rather by your own aspirations, goals, and desires? Do you see where your plans have led you and the fruit thereof? In his tender mercies and thoughtful endurance, God teaches, shows, and allows us, his children, to see the futility of our labor that is done in our own strength. Not living in accordance with his design and plan for our lives only brings us unrest and lack of peace. What are the types of things you pray for? What is the underlying reason for your prayers? Sometimes we make things harder than they are. Jesus taught us how to pray.

> "This, then, is how you should pray:
> "'Our Father in heaven,
> hallowed be your name,
> your kingdom come, your will be done, on earth as it is in heaven.
> Give us today our daily bread.
> And forgive us our debts, as we also have forgiven our debtors.
> And lead us not into temptation, but deliver us from the evil one.'"
>
> (Matthew 6:9-13)

Jesus knew how to pray. His life is also an example for us to follow. As we read how Jesus reacted to Satan's tempting, we can find faith to draw on the word of the Lord as a weapon to victoriously defeat Satan when he tempts us: "Jesus, full of the Holy Spirit, left the Jordan and was led by the Spirit into the wilderness, where for forty days he was tempted by the devil. He ate nothing during those days, and at the end of them he was hungry. The devil said to him, "If you are the Son of God, tell this stone to become bread"" (Luke

4:1-3). "Jesus answered, "It is written: 'Man shall not live on bread alone, but on every word that comes from the mouth of God'"" (Matthew 4:4).

The devil tempted him to use his supernatural powers as the Son of God for his own ends. Just as God gave the Israelites manna in a supernatural way, so we also must rely on God for spiritual nourishment as well as physical provision. Jesus relied on his Father for provision of food, not on his own miraculous power. Are you relying on your Heavenly Father for provision? Often we make a futile attempt at manipulating him with requests in the form of prayer, all the while wondering why we do not receive an answer.

> The devil led him up to a high place and showed him in an instant all the kingdoms of the world. And he said to him, "I will give you all their authority and splendor; it has been given to me, and I can give it to anyone I want to. If you worship me, it will be all yours." Jesus answered, "It is written: "Worship the Lord your God and serve him only."
>
> The devil led him to Jerusalem and had him stand on the highest point of the temple. "If you are the Son of God," he said, "throw yourself down from here. For it is written: "'He will command his angels concerning you to guard you carefully; they will lift you up in their hands, so that you will not strike your foot against a stone.'" Jesus answered: "It is said: 'Do not put the Lord your God to the test.'"
>
> When the devil had finished all this tempting, he left him until an opportune time. (Luke 4:5-13)

Jesus did not accomplish his mission by using his supernatural power for his own needs. He did not try to win a large following by performing miracles or by compromising with Satan. Being God, Jesus had no inward inclination to sin, although the temptation was real and he was confronted with genuine opportunity to sin. He defeated the tempter with a weapon everyone has at their disposal and described in Ephesians 6:17, "the sword of the Spirit, which is the word of God."

The testing of Jesus was intentional. The testing of his chosen people was intentional as well. The Lord led the Israelites in the desert for forty years. Of this time, Moses recounted God's faithfulness while conveying a vital message from the Lord to the people:

> Be careful to follow every command I am giving you today, so that you may live and increase and may enter and possess the land that the LORD promised on oath to your ancestors. Remember how the LORD your God led you all the way in the wilderness these forty years, to humble you and to test you in order to know what was in your heart, whether or not you would keep his commands. He humbled you, causing you to hunger and then feeding you with manna, which neither you nor your ancestors had known, to teach you that man does not live on bread alone but on every word that comes from the mouth of the LORD. (Deuteronomy 8:1-3)

At the beginning of Jesus' ministry, he was subjected to a similar test and showed himself to be the true Israelite who lives on every word that comes from the mouth of the Lord. Adam failed the test and plunged the human race into sin. Jesus, however, was faithful and demonstrated his qualification to become the Savior of all who receive him. It was important that Jesus was tested and tempted as Israel was, and as we are, so that he could become our merciful and faithful high priest; able to help us when we are tempted. As Jesus was faithful in resisting temptation, he became a model for all believers when they are tempted by the devil.

Like the Hebrew for Satan, the Greek word for *devil* means accuser or slanderer. Sin will trick you and trap you; and then Satan will accuse you, causing guilt. There is no need for you to walk around guilty when you are given a free exemption through Jesus Christ. All you have to do is ask! In light of this exemption, why would anyone want to walk around feeling guilty? You do not need to walk that path. Just turn around and go the other way! Repent while it is still today. Humble yourself under God's hand and be submissive to him. If you truly act in this way, God himself will move mightily on your behalf. You will then begin to walk in his kingdom and glory, and walk a life of faith.

"Consider it pure joy, my brothers and sisters, whenever you face trials of many kinds, because you know that the testing of your faith produces perseverance. Let perseverance finish its work so that you may be mature and complete, not lacking anything" (James 1:2-4). Our behavior should be in keeping with how God would have us react at all costs.

"When tempted, no one should say, "God is tempting me." For God cannot be tempted by evil, nor does he tempt anyone; but each person is tempted when they are dragged away by their own evil desire and enticed" (James 1:13-14).

We will be tempted repeatedly in life. We will have to pass the testing of our faith. Without faith, it is impossible to please God. Think about this when you are making decisions or reacting to someone or a situation. Do you want to please God or man, the Creator or the created? Do you serve God or man? If you serve God you will automatically become a servant to man.

Jesus served, and as followers of him, we are likewise to serve. A good example of service is given in the instructions for deacons. The Greek word for *deacon* means simply *one who serves*. Here are the instructions for deacons: "He must also have a good reputation with outsiders, so that he will not fall into disgrace and into the devil's trap. In the same way, deacons are to be worthy of respect, sincere, not indulging in much wine, and not pursuing dishonest gain. They must keep hold of the deep truths of the faith with a clear conscience. They must first be tested; and then if there is nothing against them, let them serve as deacons. In the same way, the women are to be worthy of respect, not malicious talkers but temperate and trustworthy in everything. A deacon must be faithful to his wife and must manage his children and his household well" (1 Timothy 3:7-12). This sounds like an outline for servant living. I cannot help but think of the many people in these positions in churches whose behavior is contrary to that instruction. Many times they have simply failed the test. Jesus called those who act like this "whitewashed tombs."

Jesus said, "For many are invited, but few are chosen" (Matthew 22:14). It is God's will that none perish. Many are invited to be part of his kingdom. However, the invitation must first be accepted and then followed with appropriate conduct. Proper behavior is evidence of being chosen.

John was a forerunner for Christ. The old had to be removed before the new could be established. "In those days John the Baptist came, preaching in the wilderness of Judea and saying, "Repent for the kingdom of heaven has come near"" (Matthew 3:1-2). It is the same principle at work in us when we repent; we accept Jesus Christ as our Lord and Savior, and then allow him (through the Holy Spirit) to change us to a lifestyle suitable for kingdom living. Repentance is not just remorse or sorrow, but it is that remorse and sorrow that causes one to repent. Repentance changes an individual totally and causes them to forsake sin. A radical change in one's life as a whole is the sign of repentance, causing one to turn or return to God.

In the preaching of Jesus, and in the Gospel accounts, the kingdom of heaven (God's kingdom) is the reign that God brings about through Jesus Christ: the establishment of God's rule in the hearts and lives of his people, the overcoming of all the forces of evil, the removal from the world of all consequences of sin (including death and all that diminishes life), and the creation of a new order of righteousness and peace. All of this is free for the asking!

"And we know that in all things God works for the good of those who love him, who have been called cording to his purpose. For those God foreknew he also predestined to be conformed to the image of his

Son, that he might be the firstborn among many brothers and sisters. And those he predestined, he also called; those he called, he also justified; those he justified, he also glorified" (Romans 8:28-30). Are you hearing the call?

CHAPTER 3

CONSCIOUSNESS AND CONSEQUENCES

When you are put in a position to act or in a situation to react, you can do the right thing and make the right choice. If you do not do what is right, you will have a guilty conscience. Not necessarily just around people who cannot see inward reactions, but before God who sees both your outward actions and knows what is in your heart. Two wrongs never make anything right. I have seen a bitter thing: Someone will try to vindicate their actions by trying to discredit another person in order to appease their own guilty conscience. Because they have done something wrong or harbor envy within their heart, they try to divert the attention to another person by attempting to make them look bad. Herein is born slander and lies and, oftentimes, where factions develop.

"So I strive always to keep my conscience clear before God and man" (Acts 24:16). *The American Heritage Dictionary* defines *conscience* as *the faculty of recognizing the distinction between right and wrong in regard to one's conduct coupled with a sense that one should act accordingly.* Jesus said, "When the Advocate comes, whom I will send to you from the Father – the Spirit of truth who goes out from the Father – he will testify about me" (John 15:26). "When he comes, he will prove the world to be in the wrong about sin and righteousness and judgment" (John 16:8).

"There is a way that appears to be right, but in the end it leads to death" (Proverbs 14:12). Conscience is a reliable guide only when enlightened by the Holy Spirit. The word of the Lord is the truth that the Holy Spirit will call to our remembrance as we need to apply it to our everyday life or situations.

> The law of the LORD is perfect, refreshing the soul. The statutes of the LORD are trustworthy, making wise the simple. The precepts of the LORD are right, giving joy to the heart. The commands of the LORD are radiant, giving light to the eyes. The fear of the LORD is pure, enduring forever. The decrees of the LORD are firm, and all of them are righteous. They are more precious than gold, than much pure gold; they are sweeter than honey, than honey from the comb. By them is your servant warned; in keeping them there is great reward. Who can discern their own errors? Forgive my hidden faults. Keep your servant also from willful sins, may they not rule over me. Then I will be blameless, innocent of great transgression. (Psalm 19:7-13)

In God's mercy and loving-kindness he sent to us the Holy Spirit. Without the acceptance of the Holy Spirit, you are practicing Christianity in vain. The failure of Israel was not that she pursued the wrong thing, but that she pursued it in a futile attempt to merit God's favor by works instead of pursuing his favor by faith. God is Spirit, and if we are to follow him and walk in his ways, we need the help of the Holy Spirit. No human can keep the law in his own spirit. In fact, as stated in James 4:5, "the spirit he caused to dwell in us envies intensely." Satan appealed to that very spirit in Adam and Eve in the Garden of Eden with these deceptive words: "You will not certainly die," the serpent said to the woman. "For God knows that when you eat from it your eyes will be opened, and you will be like God, knowing good and evil" (Genesis 3:4-5). What were they thinking? What could they ever do to actually be like God?

This is a good account for us to study so that we can get a grip on reality. The reality is that we cannot or never will be like God. He created us in his image, to be imitators of him through our example, Jesus Christ. Without all the parts of the image we cannot be imitators. Impersonators act the part but are not truly imitators in their heart. A hollow tree cannot bear fruit. Bark can say all day long that it is going to bear fruit; however, this is impossible without the rest of the tree! So it is with a ritualistic approach to Christianity, not led by the Spirit. A man-made tree cannot bear fruit—neither can a man-made Christian or ministry. It has a form of God but denies the power.

"Consider therefore the kindness and sternness of God: sternness to those who fell, but kindness to you, provided that you continue in his kindness. Otherwise, you also will be cut off" (Romans 11:22). Jesus was the stone that was rejected, the rock that made them fall because of their unbelief.

> Love must be sincere. Hate what is evil; cling to what is good. Be devoted to one another in love. Honor one another above yourselves. Never be lacking in zeal, but keep your spiritual fervor, serving the Lord. Be joyful in hope, patient in affliction, faithful in prayer. Share with the Lord's people who are in need. Practice hospitality. Bless those who persecute you; bless and do not curse. Rejoice with those who rejoice; mourn with those who mourn. Live in harmony with one another. Do not be proud, but be willing to associate with people of low position. Do not be conceited.
>
> Do not repay anyone evil for evil. Be careful to do what is right in the eyes of everyone. If it is possible, as far as it depends on you, live at peace with everyone. Do not take revenge, my dear friends, but leave room for God's wrath, for it is written: "It is mine to avenge; I will repay," says the Lord. On the contrary: "If your enemy is hungry, feed him; if he is thirsty, give him something to drink. In doing this, you will heap burning coals

on his head." Do not be overcome by evil, but overcome evil with good.

Let everyone be subject to the governing authorities, for there is no authority except that which God has established. The authorities that exist have been established by God. Consequently, whoever rebels against the authority is rebelling against what God has instituted, and those who do so will bring judgment on themselves. For rulers hold no terror for those who do right, but for those who do wrong. Do you want to be free from fear of the one in authority? Then do what is right and you will be commended. For the one in authority is God's servant for your good. But if you do wrong, be afraid, for rulers do not bear the sword for no reason. They are God's servants, agents of wrath to bring punishment on the wrongdoer. Therefore, it is necessary to submit to the authorities, not only because of possible punishment but also as a matter of conscience. This is also why you pay taxes, for the authorities are God's servants, who give their full time to governing. Give to everyone what you owe them: If you owe taxes, pay taxes; if revenue, then revenue; if respect, then respect; if honor, then honor.

Let no debt remain outstanding, except the continuing debt to love one another, for whoever loves others has fulfilled the law. The commandments, "You shall not commit adultery," "You shall not murder," "You shall not steal," "You shall not covet," and whatever other commandment there may be, are summed up in this one command: "Love your neighbor as yourself." Love does no harm to neighbor. Therefore love is the fulfillment of the law. And do this, understanding the present time. The hour has come for you to wake up from your slumber, because our salvation is nearer now than when we first believed. (Romans 12:9 - 13:8-11)

The Day and Hour Unknown

But about that day or hour no one knows, not even the angels in heaven, nor the Son, but only the Father. As it was in the days of Noah, so it will be at the coming of the Son of Man. For in the days before the flood, people were eating and drinking, marrying and giving in marriage, up to the day Noah entered the ark; and they knew nothing about what would happen until the flood came and took them all away. That is how it will be at the coming of the Son of Man. Two men will be in the field; one will be taken and the other left. Two women will be grinding with a hand mill; one will be taken and the other left. "Therefore keep watch, because you do not know on what day your Lord will come." (Matthew 24:36-42)

At that time the kingdom of heaven will be like ten virgins who took their lamps and went out to meet the bridegroom. Five of them were foolish and five were wise. The foolish ones took their lamps but did not take any oil with them. The wise ones, however, took oil in jars along with their lamps. The bridegroom was a long time in coming, and they all became drowsy and fell asleep. "At midnight the cry rang out: 'Here's the bridegroom! Come out to meet him!' "Then all the virgins woke up and trimmed their lamps. The foolish ones said to the wise, 'Give us some of your oil; our lamps are going out.' "'No,' they replied, 'there may not be enough for both us and you. Instead, go to those who sell oil and buy some for yourselves.' "But while they were on their way to buy the oil, the bridegroom arrived. The virgins who were ready went in with him to the wedding banquet. And the door was shut." (Matthew 25:1-10)

For you know very well that the day of the Lord will come like a thief in the night. While people are saying "Peace and safety," destruction will come on them suddenly, as labor pains on a pregnant woman, and they will not escape. But you, brothers and sisters, are not in darkness so that this day should surprise you like a thief. You are all children of the light and children of the day. We do not belong to the night or to the darkness. So then, let us not be like others, who are asleep, but let us be awake and sober. (1 Thessalonians 5:2-6)

For you were once darkness, but now you are light in the Lord. Live as children of light (for the fruit of the light consists in all goodness, righteousness and truth) and find out what pleases the Lord. Have nothing to do with the fruitless deeds of darkness, but rather expose them. It is shameful even to mention what the disobedient do in secret. But everything exposed by the light becomes visible – and everything that is illuminated becomes a light. This is why it is said: "Wake up, O sleeper, rise from the dead, and Christ will shine on you." Be very careful, then, how you live—not as unwise but as wise, making the most of every opportunity, because the days are evil. Therefore do not be foolish, but understand what the Lord's will is. Do not get drunk on wine, which leads to debauchery. Instead, be filled with the Spirit. (Ephesians 5:8-18)

Walking in the Spirit

The filling of the Spirit is not a onetime event that automatically sanctifies an individual or equips them for all experiences, exempting them from any effort of their own. The Spirit empowers us to live a Christ like life here on earth in evil times, in an evil environment. The Spirit repeatedly empowers, enables, and prompts us to accomplish God's will and purpose for our lives. However, we choose to submit to any influence that affects us, thereby choosing to heed the Spirit's prompting.

Our old lifestyle resulted from deceitful desires that brought about destructive behavior. This is why we have to put off our old self and walk in newness of life in a lifestyle God desires so that he can produce in us the fruit of the Holy Spirit. Therefore, we have to be sensitive to the prompting and conviction of the Spirit who works God's will and purpose for our lives.

We have an opportunity to live in the light and walk in the light. We can be sensitive and not harden our hearts to the truth of the Word of God, no matter what the circumstance or appearance of the circumstance may be. You can learn to trust and love God with your whole heart, mind, spirit, soul, and body, and submit your whole being in obedience to him. You are not controlled by the sinful nature, but by the Spirit if the Spirit of God lives in you. You have an obligation, but not to the sinful nature. A Spirit controlled life is the fruit of the presence of the Holy Spirit in our lives.

> The Spirit himself testifies with our spirit that we are God's children. Now if we are children, then we are heirs—heirs of God and co-heirs with Christ, if indeed we share in his sufferings in order that we may also share in his glory. I consider that our present sufferings are not worth comparing with the glory that will be revealed in us. (Romans 8:16-18)

> Therefore, since Christ suffered in his body, arm yourselves also with the same attitude, because he who suffers in the body is done with sin. As a result, they do not live the rest of their earthly lives for evil human desires, but rather for the will of God. (1 Peter 4:1-2)

As believers, we are to be prepared to suffer unjustly and face such abuse with Christ's attitude, which is to forgive those who do us harm (for chances are, they do not know what they are doing). Suffering can enable us to straighten out our priorities. Sinful desires and practices that once seemed important become insignificant when one's life is in jeopardy. Serious suffering for Christ advances the progress of sanctification.

"And we know that in all things God works for the good of those who love him, who have been called according to his purpose. For those

God foreknew he also predestined to be conformed to the image of his Son, that he might be the firstborn among many brothers and sisters. And those he predestined, he also called; those he called, he also justified; those he justified, he also glorified" (Romans 8:28-30).

Obstacles and Obstructions in the Path

"As is written in the book of the words of Isaiah the prophet: "A voice of one calling in the wilderness, 'Prepare the way for the Lord, make straight paths for him. Every valley shall be filled in, every mountain and hill made low. The crooked roads shall become straight, the rough ways smooth. And all people will see God's salvation'" (Luke 3:4-6).

In ancient times, before a king made a journey to a distant country, the roads he would travel were improved. Similarly, preparation for the Messiah was made in a moral and spiritual way by the ministry of John, which focused on repentance, forgiveness of sin, and the need for a Savior. Jesus' saving work on the cross was necessary before sending the Holy Spirit. He said, "But very truly I tell you, it is for your good that I am going away. Unless I go away, the Advocate will not come to you; but if I go, I will send him to you. When he comes, he will prove the world to be in the wrong about sin and righteousness and judgment" (John 16:7-8).

Apart from the Spirit's convicting work, people can never see themselves as sinners, or envision that a righteous status before God does not depend on good works, but on Christ's redemptive work on the cross. A total moral renewal manifests itself in righteous living. Righteous living encompasses all aspects of life. What you do at home is as important as what you do at work, which is as important as what you do with your social life, which is as important as how you act at church.

"'Love the Lord your God with all your heart and with all your soul and with all your mind and with all your strength.' The second is this: 'Love your neighbor as yourself.'" There is no commandment greater than these" (Mark 12:30-31). If you live like this, you are obeying the laws and precepts of the Lord. However, if you obey only laws or only precepts, this is of no eternal value. Being religious has no eternal value. If you do great humanitarian works, even these have no eternal value in and of themselves. If you do all these things and harbor anything less than love, they are of no value. Jesus is the one who makes the final decision about a person's eternal destiny, and he said: "Not everyone who says to me, 'Lord, Lord,' will enter the kingdom of heaven, but only the one who does the will of my Father who is in heaven. Many will say to me on that day, 'Lord, Lord, did we not prophesy in your name and in your name drive out demons and in your name perform many miracles?' Then I will tell them plainly, 'I never knew you. Away from me, you evildoers!'" (Matthew 7:21-23). "Enter through the narrow gate. For wide is the gate and broad is the road that leads to destruction, and many enter through it. But small is the gate and narrow the road that leads to life, and only a few find it" (Matthew 7:13-14).

As stated in Psalm 23:3: "he refreshes my soul. He guides me along the right paths for his name's sake." As a shepherd leads his sheep in paths that offer safety and well-being, God leads us in his moral will for our lives through the prompting and conviction of the Holy Spirit, guiding us to safe paths, well-being, and in ways that cause us to be secure and prosperous. He clears obstacles out of our path, leaving nothing for us to stumble over. This clearing is a process that requires work on our behalf, and we are accountable to do it.

"I urge you, brothers and sisters, to watch out for those who cause divisions and put obstacles in your way that are contrary to the teaching you have learned. Keep away from them. For such people are not serving our Lord Christ, but their own appetites. By smooth talk and flattery they deceive the minds of naive people" (Romans 16:17-18). "Do not be misled: "Bad company corrupts good character"" (1 Corinthians 15:33). Putting the application of these words into action in our lives will make our walk much smoother.

"If you say, "The LORD is my refuge," and you make the Most High your dwelling, no harm will overtake you, no disaster will come near your tent. For he will command his angels concerning you to guard you in all your ways; they will lift you up in their hands, so that you will not strike your foot against a stone. You will tread upon the lion and the cobra; you will trample the great lion and the serpent" (Psalm 91:9-13). Please examine this passage carefully. You will be guarded in all your ways, not wants. At times, our wants are to our spiritual detriment.

The angels, (messengers of God) will lift you up and quite possibly out of a situation or into one so that you will not strike your foot against a stone (obstacle in your path).

Part of the definition of *tread* means *to trample so as to press, crush, or injure*. Think about this. Some situations we get into become pressing, and at times we almost feel crushed or injured by circumstances. Now make the application spiritually. The Lord causes us to be victorious by treading on the great lion. Who prowls about like a roaring lion seeking whom he may devour? That great lion is Satan. We may have gotten ourselves into a trap of Satan, who would like to devour us through where the situation is leading us.

Remember that God's ways are higher. So when we feel undeservingly pressed out of a situation or into one, crushed or injured in it, we must remember in whose hands we are. You will be lifted up so as not to be harmed by the obstacle with which the serpent is trying to trick you. This is the power and backup we have as believers and followers of Christ. For he himself said: "I have given you authority to trample on snakes and scorpions and to overcome all the power of the enemy; nothing will harm you" (Luke 10:19). The snakes and scorpions may represent evil spirits (Satan's henchmen), and the enemy is Satan.

Love is very powerful, especially fourfold love (heart, mind, soul and strength) which requires total devotion. "And so we know and rely on the love God has for us. God is love. Whoever lives in love lives in God, and God in them" (1 John 4:16). So if we live in God, then he is our dwelling place and the promises are ours. Perfect love casts out fear and genuine love is never self-generated by God's creatures, but ultimately comes through God and in God.

The fact that we are like Christ in love is a sign that God, who is love, lives in us. So no matter what the consequence or what trial we may face, we have confidence in God and his Word that he will work all things together for our good, whether we can see it or not, if we are sincere. "Because he loves me," says the LORD, "I will rescue him; I will protect him, for he acknowledges my name. He will call on me and I will answer him; I will be with him in trouble, I will deliver him and honor him. With long life I will satisfy him and show him my salvation"" (Psalm 91:14-16).

"For he chose us in him before the creation of the world to be holy and blameless in his sight. In love" (Ephesians 1:4). This is a divine election by grace. Holiness and sanctification are imparted to us because of Christ. Keep in mind that sanctification is a process. "Whoever loves discipline loves knowledge, but whoever who hates correction is stupid" (Proverbs 12:1). "For God does speak—now one way, now another—though no one perceives it" (Job 33:14). As we grow in knowledge and depth of insight we are able to discern what is best. We know that God is in control and we strive to become filled with the fruit of righteousness, trusting him; "being confident of this, that he who began a good work in you will carry it on to completion until the day of Christ Jesus" (Philippians 1:6).

God may be trying to get your attention or actually speaking to you through your circumstance. We need the Holy Spirit, our Advocate, to lead, guide, and direct us into all truth, and we need to be submissive to his leading and direction, and heed God's correction. The Lord is my shepherd, and his rod and staff comfort me in correction, discipline, and often at times, through circumstances and events. He leads us and we either follow or go in another direction, to our detriment. If we do not return from that wrong direction, ultimately, our destruction is inevitable.

Satan comes to rob; he would like to steal the blessing of God from you. He is destructive in his design sets that are always contrary to Gods. He comes to destroy and kill. If you are not strong in the Lord and in his mighty power, and if you take off any part of the full armor of God, you most likely will not be able to stand against the devil's schemes. As explained in Ephesians 6:13-18, the armor God gives us is the belt of truth, the breastplate of righteousness, the shield of faith, the helmet of salvation, and the sword of the Spirit, which is the Word of God. With that armor on, we are to stand firm on our feet that must be fitted with the readiness that comes from the gospel of peace, the word of God. We must then remain self-controlled, alert, and pray in the Spirit on all occasions.

Keep in mind that the battle is spiritual and must be fought in God's strength, depending on him through prayer, while heeding the prompting of the Holy Spirit. On all occasions we must keep on praying for all the saints (our brothers and sisters in Christ) God commands us to love. What are occasions? Occasions are events such as wrong being done to us, sickness, disaster, heartache or loss, persecution, or whatever trial that presents itself in our lives. At these times, we must seek God's advice through prayer, praying also for our brothers and sisters who may be enduring the same things. We need to heed warnings and signs that we may have been knocked off track and God may be trying to get our attention.

Whatever the obstacles are, that prevent us from walking on the smooth, straight and narrow path; the best thing for us to do is remove them. We need to examine the road we are on to find the crooked ways, rough spots, low areas, or mountains of things we have put above the way God wants us to walk. When we find them in our lives, we must repair our way. When the conviction of the Holy Spirit comes, it is time to lighten the load for travel and make the road conditions better, but we must follow his prompting and calling to do so. You never know. It may be his last warning or final call before you fall off your mountain, get flooded in your valley, are lost in your crooked way, or are found struggling in your rough way, allowing your love for him and others to grow cold. When the end of your walk comes, which path do you want to be found on: God's narrow path that leads to eternal life, or the broad path that allows you to carry a lot of baggage with you as it leads you to destruction? We need to deal drastically with sin before sin drastically deals with us.

"From the days of John the Baptist until now, the kingdom of heaven has been subjected to violence, and violent people have been raiding it" (Matthew 11:12). Think about treading on the lion and serpent and that *tread means to trample press, crush or injure*. Jesus taught the necessity of dealing drastically with sin. He said, "If your right eye causes you to stumble, gouge it out and throw it away. It is better for you to lose one part of your body than for your whole body to be thrown into hell. And if your right hand causes you to stumble, cut it off and throw it away. It is better for you to lose one part of your body than for your whole body to go into hell" (Matthew 5:29-30). Prior to saying this, he was talking about how obeying the law is more than just taking physical action or outward obedience. He made the point that within our heart and thoughts lay our true intents and motives, and God knows them all. If one looks lustfully at someone, he said, one has already committed adultery in one's heart. How do we stop this from happening? Stop looking! Turn your head! Change the television channel! Stop reading it! Stop hanging around those places! Stop hanging around those people! Do whatever it takes to remove the obstacle that could cause you to stumble. If you are convicted, now is the time to make the change. If you are suffering some unpleasant consequences, ask your Heavenly Father. He will show you what you need to do to remove the obstacle from your path.

CHAPTER 4

HERE'S YOUR SIGN

Jesus said this about signs of the end of the age: "Now learn this lesson from the fig tree: As soon as its twigs get tender and its leaves come out, you know that summer is near. Even so when you see all these things, you know that it is near, right at the door" (Matthew 24:32-33). The types of things he referred to were wars and rumors of wars, nations rising against one another, earthquakes, famines, fearful events, the appearance of false prophets, and the increase of wickedness which will cause the love of most to grow cold. "But mark this: There will be terrible times in the last days. People will be lovers of themselves, lovers of money, boastful, proud, abusive, disobedient to their parents, ungrateful, unholy, without love, unforgiving, slanderous, without self-control, brutal, not lovers of the good, treacherous, rash, conceited, lovers of pleasure rather than lovers of God—having a form of godliness but denying its power. Have nothing to do with such people" (2 Timothy 3:1-5).

Just look at some of the recent news highlights. Many of these things are happening in increasing intensity in places where they have never before happened. They are falling into the line of events that Jesus told us would happen.

Here Are Some Recent News Headlines

Pestilences, Hurricanes, Typhoons, Floods, Earthquakes, Tornados, Uprisings, Mass Murders, Terrorist Attacks, Beheadings, Persecutions, Increasing Persecution of Christians, Loss of Christian Rights, Wars, Civil Wars, Nations against Nations, Oppression, Robbery, Murder, Abductions, Perversions, Hostages Held, Hate Crimes, Children Suing Parents, Rebellions, Removal of Prayer from Schools, Legalization of Abortion, Institution of Gay Marriage, Ethical Failure, Political Scandals and Financial Crisis. There is an increased effort to take Christ out of Christmas and society in general. People are offended by the cross and the mention of Jesus Christ.

The United States of America is a nation founded under God, with liberty and freedom and justice for all. So what has happened? I believe that all that has happened is due to compromise. The same things going on now have happened throughout the history of God's people. Kings and leaders lead people astray by teaching them to compromise, promoting beliefs that are contrary to God's instructions for a life of blessing. Every time this happened in the history of the Old Testament it brought disaster. The United States may have been founded as a nation under God, but it is turning away from living under God's rule and making up its own. This is a terrible mistake on behalf of its leaders.

As confessing Christians, only we are without excuse because we have the entire Old Testament to read as well as the New Testament. When one is removed from under God's authoritative rule, the blessing is removed as well. Something terrible is happening; Christians are being singled out in the workplace and in society in general. As immorality gains ground in the United States and given more rights, I believe we are going to see the persecution of Christians intensify. As this begins to happen, many will become fearful, compromise, and give up on standing on the promises of God. They will forfeit their rights to the kingdom by no longer applying kingdom principles to their lives. For example, if the government decides to no longer allow tax exemptions for charitable donations to churches, this may influence many Christians to neglect the principle of tithing, to their detriment, causing them to forfeit the blessings that come from obedience to that principle.

There is another insidious trend I see taking hold in the United States: It is okay to wear a T-shirt with a devil or demonic image on it, but not one with a scripture, an image of Jesus Christ, or the cross. No one is radically, publicly expressing their offense with all the demonic paraphernalia that is displayed everywhere and not just at Halloween, yet they are offended by the display of a cross at Easter, or a manger scene at Christmas.

Whether on television or the Internet, television shows (including children's cartoons), movies, reading materials, and most other entertainment activities are increasingly filled with lewd, demonic, and violent images and behavior. Somehow this is all becoming acceptable. Even pornography is being accepted as normal by many adults. Television commercials and ads are enough to make you blush. We can sum all this up in one word: unholy.

Society condones and accepts immoral behavior as normal. The United States is no longer united, but becoming more and more divided. She is no longer one nation under God. She has compromised her original beliefs. She has set herself, her knowledge, and her wisdom above God and His knowledge and wisdom. Her idols have risen up, above God. This is not good.

Worse yet is the church's compromise with immorality. There is a division in the church over religious doctrines. A house divided cannot stand. The church is being made a mockery due to the hypocritical lifestyle lived by so many who claim to be a part of her, who have lost the power and ability to be a true witness. Compromise is a dangerous snare. It causes many to cling to religion rather than Christianity. Many wolves in sheep's clothing and false prophets have infiltrated the church, appealing to the lusts of the flesh in weak-minded, unstable believers, leading them down a perverted path away from the truth, taking advantage of them.

We are seeing tornados and floods in places we have never seen them before. We have experienced terror in the United States unlike ever before. We have seen the moon turned to blood. There has been bloodshed and fire. There are signs in the heavens and signs on the earth that we are in the end times. God warned us these things were going to happen. Have you considered all these warning signs? The following poem was written after a horrific event.

HURRICANE ISABELLE

*Those who are wise have no cause to fear,
For judgment time is drawing near.
The whispers in the wind have made it clear,
For judgment time is drawing near.
The hour, the day, the time we do not know,
But of this we can be sure, we will reap what we sow
The fruits of our labors,
How we treat our neighbors.
Judgment in the land
With one sweep of his hand.
A sign for the wise
For no one can disguise
What lies within the heart
Which is deceitful from the start.
You must want to learn
From wicked ways to turn.
To live in the light
And to do what is right.
If you lie cheat and connive
You will find that all you derive
Is not there that you sought after
In life ever after,
That goes on forever.*

For the wise and the clever
No tricks there, just treats
But you have already earned your eats
In the life that you've once to live
This may be the last time the wind will give.
The opportunity while you are still alive
Into God's forgiveness to dive
And come out washed and clean and new
With a new purpose in life or to renew
The one that you may have lost
Before all eternity it will cost
Living in the dark
With the lost.
(Kathleen Poulton—September 30, 2003)

Hurricane Isabelle Possibly a Warning Bell Some Food for Thought

The world and its ways can very easily conquer you, by influencing you to lean to an earthly, unspiritual way of thinking. How? Through unforgiveness, loss of love, fear, and moral compromise. Always keep in mind that no one act of disobedience to God's Word is worse than any other. There have even been acts of hate done under the guise of Christianity that have been anything but Christ like. I am saying this because of the increase of wickedness in the world, so that you do not fall into an attitude of judgment and become cynical. This is also something about which Jesus warned us: The love of most would grow cold because of the increase of wickedness. Sin is sin. Sin separates people from God. However, we are to love people as God loved us while we were yet sinners. We are to hate the sin, not the people.

There is a spiritual battle going on to conquer our great nation, the United States of America. This battle threatens to dethrone her of her great power, abundance, and peace. There is a war against Christianity and the church, an attempt to leave her powerless, defeated, or ultimately, conquer her. The application of the definition of *conquer* used here is, *to overcome by mental or moral force*. Compromise is the vice in action. The mind governed by the flesh is death, but the mind governed by the Spirit is life and peace, and a nation under God's authority is a great place of abundance and peace.

Disobedient hesitation can cost you your life. Is it worth it to put off to tomorrow what you know that you should do today? Today, if you hear God's voice, it is time to react. If he tells you to stop doing this or that, to go a certain way, or to leave a place, obey his prompting, knowing it is for your good. It may be the last time you will hear the call.

God has already told us in his Word that the earth will see Jesus coming on the clouds of the sky with power and great glory. He will send his angels with a loud trumpet call and they will gather his elect. He told us that two would be working together and that one would be taken and the other left behind. It could happen at any time.

Immorality in the United States is nearing the levels of Sodom and Gomorrah. *Sodom* actually means *a low level of morality*. Just as Lot and his family were warned, I believe God is warning the church to come out from the increasingly immoral lifestyle of our society to live separately.

The story of Sodom and Gomorrah and what happened to them and their inhabitants is enlightening.

> So Lot went out and spoke to his sons-in-law, who were pledged to marry his daughters. He said, "Hurry and get out of this place, because the LORD is about to destroy the city!" But his sons-in-law thought he was joking. With the coming of dawn, the angels urged Lot, saying, "Hurry! Take your wife and your two daughters who are here, or you will be swept away when the city is punished." When he hesitated, the men grasped his hand and the hands of his wife and of his two daughters and led them safely out of the city. The Lord was merciful to them. (Genesis 19:14-16)

Psalm 91:11 says, "For he will command his angels concerning you in all your ways."Out of God's mercy toward us he leads us in paths of righteousness for his name's sake. Consider that a path to which God has led you may well be one that keeps you from danger and destruction. Sometimes when we hesitate, he has to take hold of us. Lot may have hesitated because he was reluctant to leave behind his material possessions. However, due to God's mercy on him and his family, God gave his angels charge of them. The angels then took charge of the situation and physically grasped the hands of Lot and his family and led them to safety.

This same principle applies when we hesitate and God needs to move us to a safe place. If we do not willingly move as quickly as we should, he can arrange events and circumstances or remove things or people to move us into a place of eternal safety. Moving us or removing something or someone from us may give us a different view of an event and cause us to reevaluate the direction or path we have been walking. The path we were on may have been a wide one leading to destruction, and we may have been carrying some harmful baggage that held us back from entering the narrow path. In helping us work out our salvation, our Heavenly Father mercifully intervenes by removing or preventing us from keeping things that would hinder us on our journey toward righteousness.

God is an ever-present help in times of distress. Therefore, those of us who truly love our Heavenly Father must trust him, as he knows best and has our best interests at heart. We must prayerfully thank him for where he places us, even if not a place of our choosing.

Back to the story: The Lord rained down burning sulfur on Sodom and Gomorrah and destroyed it. Perhaps this burning sulfur was from a violent earthquake, spewing up asphalt, which is still found in that region of the earth. "As soon as they had brought them out, one of them said, "Flee for your lives! Don't look back and don't stop anywhere in the plain!" Flee to the mountains or you will be swept away!" (Genesis 19:17). However, Lot's wife looked back and became a pillar of salt. That is where her disobedient hesitation landed her. Her decision was foolish, showing a lack of good sense, understanding, and foresight. When God spoke, it was for her own good. Why would she look back on immoral actions and behavior? What do you suppose was the attraction?

There are grotesque salt formations near the southern end of the Dead Sea that are reminders of Lot's wife's folly: a reminder to us of what unbelief can cost. Today, if you hear his voice, do not harden your heart. Heed the call.

CHAPTER 5

FATAL ATTRACTIONS

Why do you make the decisions that you make? What are the reasons that you elect people to governing positions? Do you vote for officials who appeal to the lusts of your flesh who appeal to wrong and deceitful desires of your heart? Do you vote one into a leadership position because of the political party that he or she belongs to or because of the color of their skin, even if his agenda is to compromise with the world and is contrary to God's decrees, ordinances and principles? Do you make decisions because of harbored prejudices and unforgiveness? Do you covet, act or react out of craftiness, self-centeredness, and ungratefulness, love of money, greed, and pride? What about accountability? Do you find yourself participating in gossip making slanderous remarks, repeating things that someone told you in confidence thereby betraying that person for a self centered selfish reason of your own? Because you feel incompetent do you try to cause others to think less of someone whom you are jealous and envious of? If you are wronged do you seek to cause harm back? Do two wrongs ever make anything right? Wrong is wrong and right is right! What are we condoning? What are we going along with? Are we concerned that we may not be popular if we do not participate in something that the Holy Spirit is convicting us not to do because of fear of rejection by a person or persons? Have you been reacting out of fears that you have been carrying with you from past experiences of being wronged or rejected? A root of unforgiveness can grow into a vine that branches into areas of our life that cause us to react in an unfaithful or disobedient way that is contrary to the precepts and statutes of God fatally attracting us to do the wrong thing or go the wrong way. It is for freedom that Christ has set us free, so that we are not burdened by a yoke of oppression.

So many bad choices, wrong decisions, harbored ill emotions and thoughts and deceitful ways that are harmful to others and to us could be avoided by practicing the teachings of Jesus and living according to God's words.

THE CHOICE

To know and obey can keep you out of harm's way
For we have the Holy Spirit to help us today
And from his guidance we do not sway.
From the very words of God that he brings to our mind
Every test and trial we can leave behind.
All of the emotions and events meant to bind
And at day's end we unwind,
And lay them at the feet of our Lord
Who enables us in battle as we pick up our sword.
Then run to win at new day's dawn
For you have seen the light shed on the darkness pawn
And in kingdom power you move on.
The heavenly light begins to dawn,
The flaunting darkness is overcome
The celebration of victory has begun.
God's abundant provision you see as best
Living a life here in peace and at rest
Hidden in Christ Jesus who in his love has blessed
Us with entrance while it is still today,
Through him as a door the only way
Do not harden your heart as wickedness you see

> *Walk in love as intended to be.*
> *In every circumstance and in any event*
> *That life here on earth to you has sent*
> *Now you can be fully content.*
> *For they are just an enablement to become*
> *One with the Father, the Holy Spirit, and Son*
> *An opportunity for others to see*
> *What your live as a witness was intended to be.*
> *(Kathleen Poulton—October 15, 2014)*

Application of God's Word in one's mind causes stability. Yielding to worldly wisdom in this or that issue or situation causes double-mindedness and leads to instability. As you are lifted to a higher level, temptations that come to you adjust to appeal to you at your level of maturity. When we first accepted Christ, the temptations we dealt with often arose from our own evil desires. If you are still enticed by those desires at the same level of temptation, you suffer unnecessarily from them and the results of yielding to them. Why? You have refused to permit your Heavenly Father to bring you into a deeper relationship with him.

It is a fact that Satan is still around, and as long as he is, it is in your best interest to be aware of it. The main device he uses against Christians is temptation. He does not stop at tempting you to sin in ways with which you are familiar, but on a deeper heart-centered, mind-set level. If he can get you to compromise or change your point of view to side with the world or its way of thinking, he has defeated you. God sometimes engineers your circumstances for your spiritual growth, to get you moving on with Jesus and his mission. It is up to you to follow God and remain faithful in everything, and not to act or react against the knowledge of God and his wisdom.

Life in Christ or Life in the Flesh

Think about this: Jesus is the bread of life. Our forefathers ate manna God gave them to sustain their physical lives. Jesus is eternal life provision. The Spirit gives life, the flesh counts for nothing. The words Jesus spoke were Spirit and life.

I find it interesting that in John 6:66, the text speaks of many of Jesus disciples turning back and no longer following him because they were not ready to receive life in the way he taught. In the book of Revelation, the beast that comes from the earth forces all to receive a mark, without which they cannot buy or sell. If you cannot buy or sell, you can no longer obtain food for physical sustenance. I find this very interesting, in that those who do not receive and partake of Jesus Christ (and of him being the bread of life) will be left behind and subjected to this. Notice also that beast's number: 666, or man's number. Man is nothing but flesh without the Spirit. Flesh is not eternal.

You, however, do not have to wait to be subjected to that decision. You can decide now who you will be ruled by; the flesh and man or the Spirit and Jesus Christ. "If any of you lacks wisdom, you should ask God, who gives generously to all without finding fault, and it will be given to you. But when you ask, you must believe and not doubt, because the one who doubts is like a wave of the sea, blown and tossed by the wind. That person should not expect to receive anything from the Lord. Such a person is double-minded and unstable in all they do" (James 1:5-8). Whose affection are you looking to gain? The world's or God's? Remember how Jesus summed up the law: "'Love the Lord your God with all your heart and with all your soul and with all your mind and with all your strength.' The second is this: 'Love your neighbor as yourself.' There is no commandment greater than these" (Mark 12:30-31).

David who was a man after God's own heart prayed like this: "Oh, how I love your law! I meditate on it all day long. Your commands are always with me and make me wiser than my enemies. I have more insight than all my teachers, for I meditate on your statutes. I have more understanding than the elders, for I obey your precepts. I have kept my feet from every evil path so that I might obey your word" (Psalm 119:97-101). "I obey your statutes, for I love them greatly. I obey your precepts and your statutes, for all my ways are known to you" (Psalm 119:167-168).

A statute is a law enacted by a legislature. A decree is an authoritative order having the force of law, often given by a ruler.

An edict is a proclamation having the force of a law, issued by an authority. A precept is a rule or principle that imposes a particular standard of action or conduct. You are governed by whatever statutes, decrees, laws, edicts, and precepts to which you submit. If we abide in Christ, he abides in us and the Holy Spirit guides us and is our Advocate—if we yield to him and if in our standards of conduct and action we are truly trying to be Christ like.

> Therefore, there is no condemnation for those who are in Christ Jesus, because through Christ Jesus the law of the Spirit who gives life has set you free from the law of sin and death. For what the law was powerless to because it was weakened by the flesh, God did by sending his own Son in the likeness of sinful flesh to be a sin offering. And so he condemned sin in the flesh, in order that the righteous requirement of the law might be fully met in us, who do not live according to the flesh but according to the Spirit. Those who live according to the flesh have their minds set on what the flesh desires. The mind governed by the flesh is death, but the mind governed by the Spirit is life and peace. The mind governed by the flesh is hostile to God; it does not submit to God's law nor can it do so. Those who are in the realm of the flesh cannot please God. (Romans 8:1-8)

> Now if we died with Christ, we believe that we will also live with him. For we know that since Christ was raised from the dead, he cannot die again; death no longer has mastery over him. The death he died, he died to sin once for all; but the life he lives, he lives to God. In the same way, count yourselves dead to sin but alive to God in Christ Jesus. Therefore do not let

sin reign in your mortal body so that you obey its evil desires. Do not offer any part of yourself to sin as an instrument of wickedness, but rather offer yourselves to God, as those who have been brought from death to life; and offer every part of yourself to him as an instrument of righteousness. For sin shall no longer be your master, because you are not under the law, but under grace. What then? Shall we sin because we are not under law but under grace? By no means! Don't you know that when you offer yourselves to someone as obedient slaves, you are slaves of the one you obey—whether you are slaves to sin, which leads to death, or to obedience, which leads to righteousness? (Romans 6:8-16)

We are to yield to Christ and offer ourselves in obedience to his teaching. His teaching sums up the whole law: Love the Lord with all your heart, soul, mind, and strength, and love your neighbor as yourself. "No one can serve two masters. Either you will hate the one and love the other, or you will be devoted to the one and despise the other. You cannot serve both God and Money" (Matthew 6:24).

Self-Sacrifice

In our worship services, we use instruments to make music to honor God. Instruments make sounds. Which parts of the body play, make, hear, and discern sounds? Hands, mouths, ears, and minds. Therefore, we are to watch what we put our hands to, what we speak, what we listen to, and how we think! "Therefore I urge you, brothers and sisters, in view of God's mercy to offer your bodies as a living sacrifice, holy and pleasing to God—this is your true and proper of worship" (Romans 12:1). "God is spirit and his worshipers must worship in the spirit and in truth" (John 4:24).

God knows what is in our hearts and judges our deeds. He knows why you do what you do and why you say what you say. "A good man brings good things out of the good stored up in him, and an evil man brings up evil things out of the evil stored up in him. But I tell you that everyone will have to give account on the day of judgment for every empty word they have spoken. For by your words you will be acquitted, and by your words you will be condemned" (Matthew 12:35-37).

The progression of spiritual life leads to sound judgment, discernment, and the ability to distinguish good from evil. There have been times in my life that were not pleasant, due to wrong choices I made. God allows us to make choices, wrong or right. We can either make good choices that lead to blessings or make wrong or bad choices and subject ourselves to suffering.

Never has there been a time when God did not answer me when I cried to him for help. Early on in my Christian walk, after I came out of a terrible situation and passed through an awful time, I saw a unique vision of myself. I was covered with mud from head to toe. When I looked into the Scriptures for insight, this is what I found: "I waited patiently for the LORD; he turned to me and heard my cry. He lifted me out of the slimy pit, out of the mud and mire; he set my feet on a rock and gave me a firm place to stand" (Psalm 40:1-2); "Husbands, love your wives, just as Christ loved the church and gave himself up for her to make her holy, cleansing her by the washing with water through the word" (Ephesians 5:25-26); "I will sprinkle clean water on you, and you will be clean; I will cleanse you from all your impurities and from all your idols. I will give you a new heart and put a new spirit in you; I will remove from you your heart of stone and give you a heart of flesh" (Ezekiel 36:25-26). Thanks be to Jesus Christ who gave himself up for me that I may be holy. He is my rock and my salvation. I cried to the Lord and he heard me and helped me to my feet. Now I am able to have my feet fitted with the word of God, the Gospel of peace. I was cleaned up by the water of the washing of the Word, through yielding to God's working and way in my life, by his Spirit. My hardness of heart has been replaced with the love of Christ.

Using Your Talents and Gifts

How are you using your gifts? Are you using your talents for your glory or for the glory of God? How do you use your authority—for your own personal gain or to assist others? Who is first in your life: you or Christ? Are you walking in *joy*: *Jesus* first, *others* second and *yourself* last? Do you consider yourself a disciple of Christ? If so, you work for him, no matter where your job is, how you are gifted, or where you are, no matter what day or time it is. If you do your work as if working for God, you will be blessed. We are to be submissive to the rulers and authorities over us, unless they tell us to do something contrary to God's Word. *It is a privilege to work for God.*

Working for Jesus means walking in the Spirit of truth who will guide us in all our ways. If you are obedient to the Word of God, you will be blessed in your coming and going, no matter what situation you are in or job you have. Read Deuteronomy 28:1-15. If you are disobedient, you bring trouble on yourself and open the door for the ruler of this world to wreak havoc in your life. I am not saying that we do not have to deal with trials, difficult people, and trouble. These are just part of living in an imperfect world with imperfect people. What I am saying is that you have the assurance that God is with you in it all if you allow him to be, and trust that if you are obedient to his Word, he will be faithful to it—all of it. When you are obedient to his Word, you will have peace, even in the midst of a storm, trial, tribulation, persecution, or wrong done to you, you will come through being blessed exceedingly and abundantly above all you could ever ask or imagine.

Always remember that wrong is never right. No matter what you are going through, if you do the right thing, you will be blessed and God himself will provide for you. However, you cannot trick God. No matter how many good deeds you may do, if you are not walking in obedience to God's Word and in the Holy Spirit, it is all vanity and in vain. True charity and generosity arise selflessly and spontaneously, as we live genuine Christian lives with no thought or plan of being noticed or repaid. This is the Christian lifestyle: Give yourself first to God, in keeping with his will, and then to others in keeping his Word active in all your ways.

Paul's letter to the church at Corinth referenced his concerns about their conduct. Since we are potentially influenced by our culture as they were, we can read his letters as instruction and inspiration. In 2 Corinthians 8:7, he said; "But since you excel in everything – in faith, in speech, in knowledge, in complete earnestness and in the love we have kindled in you – see that you also excel in this grace of giving." Out of a heart of love for Christ, we strive to do our best, as we grow in wisdom, knowledge and our continuing development of Christ-like character.

If you change and reform your ways and actions, and do not trust in deceptive words or follow evil desires, you will be blessed. You may do a lot of good deeds and attend church on a regular basis. However, your religion is false and worthless (along with your work) if you do not deal with people justly, commit adultery or perjury, harbor envy, refuse to forgive, tell lies, gossip, slander, misuse spiritual gifts or otherwise act in dishonest, detestable ways, to your own harm. Today, if you hear the voice of God calling you to reform, it is best to do so while you have the opportunity to receive his grace and mercy. You never know when it may be the last call.

The Pitfall of Pride

I have seen that one of the most fatal attractions is pride. Pride is a sense of one's own proper dignity or value, and self-respect. It is taking pleasure in one's work, achievements, or possessions, to the extent that we indulge our own self-esteem or revel in our own glory. It is demanding of its rights. Pride is good in proper perspective. It is good for us to enjoy our work when we do it to the best of our ability, and to be happy and content with our accomplishments and those of others, for we are to do our jobs as working for God.

Joseph was promoted wherever he ended up, and he used it all for God's glory. Joseph had a dream that his brother's sheaves of wheat would bow down to his sheave. After he shared this with his brothers, they were jealous of him, hated him, and could not speak a kind word to him. They plotted to kill him and stripped him of the richly ornamented robe he was wearing. They threw him into a cistern. Though his brother Judah convinced the others not to kill Joseph, they still sold him to Ishmaelites, who then took him to Egypt where he was sold to Potiphar, one of Pharaoh's officials, the captain of the guard. Throughout all of this, the Lord was with Joseph and he prospered, even while living in the house of his Egyptian master. The Lord blessed the entire household and everything Potiphar had because of Joseph.

Though Potiphar's wife continually tried to get Joseph to commit adultery with her, he continually refused. One day, she caught him by his cloak, but he ran out of the house, leaving it behind. She kept it and used it as false evidence when telling her husband a terrible lie; that Joseph had tried to take advantage of her. Her husband threw Joseph in prison. Still, the Lord was with Joseph and granted him favor in the eyes of the prison warden. He put Joseph in charge of everything to do with the prison, and he was successful in all he did. After interpreting dreams for two fellow prisoners, both former officials of Pharaoh, Joseph told one of them to remember him when he went back to work for Pharaoh. However, the man forgot about Joseph.

Two years later, Pharaoh had a dream that none of his magicians or wise men could interpret. Suddenly, the official Joseph had asked to remember him recalled Joseph, and that he had once interpreted a dream for him, in prison. He remembered that all Joseph had interpreted had come true and told this to Pharaoh. Pharaoh summoned Joseph, who interpreted his dream, predicting a coming famine. Pharaoh then put Joseph in charge of all of Egypt. God had him there to prepare for what was to come.

The famine occurred just as Joseph had predicted. Joseph's own brothers came to Egypt to obtain food. They bowed down to Joseph (just as his dream many years before had predicted). After they found out who Joseph was, they were terrified. However, Joseph extended kindness and forgiveness to them and told them not to be angry with themselves for what they had done to him because God had used the situation to preserve a remnant and save their lives through a great deliverance. Joseph then sent for his whole family, asking them to join him in Egypt, where Pharaoh gave them the best of the land to enjoy.

Never did Joseph allow his sense of dignity and self-respect to rule his decision to forgive. He did not indulge his own self-esteem by taking revenge on his brothers for the wrong they had done to him. He knew that God had fulfilled the dream he had given Joseph, and that everything he had gone through was for a greater purpose. He took true pride in his purpose to do the right thing in every situation, and was blessed exceedingly and abundantly above all that he could have asked or imagined.

Gifts that God gives us can be used for his glory, plan, and will, or our own. If used for our own, they can be fatal.

Fear Can be Fatal

Fear is another fatal attraction. Fear is the opposite of faith. Perfect love cast out fear. We are to love the Lord with all our entire heart, soul, mind, and strength. If we do, we will accomplish his will and love our neighbor as ourselves.

The soul is the animating and vital principle in man, credited with faculties of thought, action, and emotion, and often conceived as an immaterial entity. The spiritual nature of man, regarded as immortal, is separable from the body at death and susceptible to happiness or misery in a future state. It houses a person's emotional or moral nature. If you love the Lord with all your soul, even your emotions and morals are in submission to him, and are not based on reactions to the way you view life, the situations you face, or what other people do. They are not at all in accordance with the world's view or actions.

"This is how we know that we love the children of God: by loving God and carrying out his commands. In fact, this is love for God: to keep his commands. And his commands are not burdensome, for everyone born of God overcomes the world. This is the victory that has overcome the world, even our faith" (1 John 5:2-4).

"We know that we are children of God, and that the whole world is under the control of the evil one" (1 John 5:19). To overcome the world is to gain victory over its sinful pattern of life, which is another way of describing obedience to God. Such obedience is not impossible for believers because they have been born again and the Holy Spirit dwells within them and gives them strength to accomplish victory day by day.

"The LORD is my light and my salvation—whom shall I fear? The LORD is the stronghold of my life—of whom shall I be afraid? When the wicked advance against me to devour me, it is my enemies and my foes who will stumble and fall" (Psalm 27:1-2).

"Hear me, you who know what is right, you people who have taken my instruction to heart: Do not fear the reproach of mere mortals or be terrified by their insults" (Isaiah 51:7).

We should never be afraid to take a stand or to do the right thing—never. To do something wrong out of fear is not only sin, it is a lack of faith in God. Do we not believe that he will do what he said he would? God does not lie. Everything he has said will continue to come to pass. He said he would be with us to the ends of the earth. Do we believe this . . . or not?

God is the giver of gifts. He can give and he can withhold. No man can take from you what God wants you to have. God wants you to have life and to have it abundantly. When you fall into the trap of doing something wrong to protect what you have or gain some material thing, you will have a good chance of it being stolen from you anyhow and still having to give an account for your actions! Satan comes to rob, steal, and destroy. Nothing that is contrary to God's Word comes to any good for those who profess to believe in God and his Son, Jesus Christ—it is a potentially fatal attraction.

Our Choices Affect Our Future

Satan seeks to divide and conquer. Consider what happened to Lot. "And quarreling arose between Abram's herders and Lots. The Canaanites and Perizzites were also living in the land at that time. So Abram said to Lot "Let's not have any quarreling between you and me, or between your herders and mine, for we are close relatives. Is not the whole land before you? Let's part company. If you go to the left, I'll go to the right; if you go to the right, I'll go to the left"" (Genesis 13:7-9). Abram allowed Lot to choose the land he preferred. Lot looked selfishly at the land and coveted it, choosing the more picturesque and fruitful land, because of its abundant water supply. The land that he chose came close to matching Eden's ideal conditions. Abram however, would not obtain any wealth except by the Lord's blessing.

However, Lot pitched his tents near Sodom. The men of Sodom were known to be wicked. Lot was flirting with temptation by choosing to live near them. Abram, in contrast to Lot, had dealt with this entire situation selflessly, in an effort to pursue peace, according to God's will. As a result, he was abundantly blessed above anything he could ever ask or imagine. "The LORD said to Abram after Lot had parted from him, "Look around from where you are, to the north and south, to the east and west. All the land that you see I will give to you and to your offspring forever. I will make your offspring like the dust of the earth, so that if anyone could count the dust, then your offspring could be counted"" (Genesis 13:14-16). You cannot count dust.

Now consider what happened to Lot as described in the following account: Lot was living in Sodom among its wicked people, in danger due to living with filthy men of lawlessness. During a war, all the goods of Sodom and Gomorrah and all their food were carried off, along with Lot and all his possessions. When Abram heard that Lot had been taken captive, he took his trained men out in pursuit, recovered all the goods, and brought Lot back, along with his possessions, women, and other people.

"After Abram returned from defeating Kedorlaomer and the kings allied with him, the king of Sodom came out to meet him in the Valley of Shaveh (that is, the King's Valley). Then Melchizedek king of Salem brought out bread and wine. He was a priest of God Most High, and he blessed Abram, saying, "Blessed be Abram by God Most High, Creator of heaven and earth. And praise be to God Most High, who delivered your enemies into your hand." Then Abram gave him a tenth of everything" (Genesis 14:17-20). By giving Melchizedek a tenth of everything (a king's share) he was acknowledging Melchizedek's kingship and, at the same time, recognizing his blessing as a benediction from the Lord. "The king of Sodom said to Abram, "Give me the people and keep the goods for yourself." But Abram said to the king of Sodom, "With raised hand I have sworn an oath to the LORD, God Most High, Creator of heaven and earth, that I will accept nothing belonging to you, not even a thread or the strap of a sandal, so that you will never be able to say, 'I made Abram rich'" (Genesis 14:21-23). Abram would accept nothing from him which would have declared he would be indebted to him or any king but the Lord.

Faith and Obedience Bring Blessing

As you read in the above account, Abram did not harbor any bitterness toward Lot. He did not say that Lot got what he deserved since he chose to live near the devil's playground. On the contrary, he set his mind to help him. He acted in love and selflessly considered Lot above himself. Prior to all this, God spoke to Abram and told him to go to the land he would show him. Abram acted in obedience to God and left his country, his people, and his father's household. God spoke to Abram and he believed God and took him at his word, holding onto the promises of God. Abram did not concern himself with his own well-being. He had nothing to fear. God's promise to Abram had a sevenfold structure:

1. I will make you a great nation.
2. I will bless you.
3. I will make your name great.
4. You will be a blessing.
5. I will bless those who bless you.
6. Whoever curses you, I will curse.
7. All the people of the earth will be blessed through you.

Seven is the number of completion. In six days, God created the world. On the seventh day, he rested. God's promise to Abram was a complete blessing. The mission was accomplished.

> So also Abraham "believed God, and it was credited to him as righteousness." Understand, then, that those who have faith are children of Abraham. Scripture foresaw that God would justify the Gentiles by faith, and announced the gospel in advance to Abraham: "All nations will be blessed through you." So those who rely on faith are blessed along with Abraham, the man of faith. For all who rely on the works of the law are under a curse, as it is written: "Cursed is everyone who does not continue to do everything written in the Book of the Law." Clearly no one who relies on the law is justified before God, because "the righteous will live by faith." The law is not based on faith; on the contrary, it says, "The person who does these things will live by them." Christ redeemed us from the curse of the law by becoming a curse for us, for it is written: "Cursed is everyone who is hung on a pole." He redeemed us in order that the blessing given to Abraham might come to the Gentiles through Christ Jesus, so that by faith we might receive the promise of the Spirit. (Galatians 3:6-14)

A Second Chance

God bestows his Spirit upon us to enable our human spirit to do his will. This is what God had Ezekiel tell the house of Israel that he would do for them, not for their sake, but for the sake of his holy name which they had profaned among the nations:

> I will sprinkle clean water on you, and you will be clean; I will cleanse you from all your impurities and from all your idols. I will give you a new heart and put a new spirit in you; I will remove from you your heart of stone and give you a heart of flesh. And I will put my Spirit in you and move you to follow my decrees and be careful to keep my laws. Then you will live in the land I gave your ancestors; you will be my people, and I will be your God. I will save you from all your uncleanness. I will call for the grain and make it plentiful and will not bring famine upon you. I will increase the fruit of the trees and the crops of the field, so that you will no longer suffer disgrace among the nations because of famine. Then you will remember your evil ways and wicked deeds, and you will loathe yourselves for your sins and detestable practices. (Ezekiel 36:25-31)

The results of Israel's renewal were restoration to prosperity. God's undeserved grace leads to recollection and repentance. This same principle applies to us under the New Covenant. God wants to bless his people; he desires to withhold no good thing from them. They withhold the blessings themselves by following the way of Lot. However, even Lot was rescued twice by Abram. Abram prayed for Lot. We would be so blessed as to have a man of God praying for us. And we do! We have Jesus, who lives to make intercession for us, and also, more, by the Holy Spirit.

We should not give up on people. Continue to pray for them and, if possible, lead them out of harm's way. Abraham was led by, followed, and pleased God because he believed God. He took God at his word.

Why should we not take God at his word? He never changes. He is the God of love. Our Heavenly Father is the Lord of second chances. Just as the prodigal son returned home to a warm welcome to be lavishly doted upon, so it will be for those of us who do the same!

Legalists who refuse God's offer of grace and insist on pursuing righteousness through works are under a curse and under the law, because no one has ever kept the law perfectly. God's blessing has never been earned, but always been freely given. I pray for God's complete blessing in your life; that you will accomplish the mission for which you were created.

CHAPTER 6

HUMILITY AND GOD'S PROVISION

Remember the story of Job's suffering. Keep in mind all that Jesus endured on the cross. Many of us wonder when we go through tough times, heartaches, losses and other forms of suffering. We think: *Why? Why me? I am a good person. I go to church every Sunday. I tithe. I do not steal. I do not commit adultery. I do not lie. I am noble. I work hard to do my job as though working for God. I obey the law. I live my life right and do good for others. I sacrifice my time to help my family and others. I sacrifice my money or belongings for the good of others, or to help them. I support some good causes.* Have you considered that perhaps God wants to kick your spiritual life up a notch?

Has it ever gotten so bad for you that you prayed for the Lord to take you? Have all your friends and family ever deserted you? Have you suffered unto death? Imagine carrying a cross, knowing you will soon be nailed to it, after having been beaten beyond recognition. As you carry it, countless people along the way mock you and spit at you, though you have done nothing but heal them, minister to them, love them, and tell them the truth. Jesus said, "Whoever does not take up their cross and follow me is not worthy of me" (Matthew 10:38).

Consider Job's test:

> Then the LORD said to Satan, "Have you considered my servant Job? There is no one on earth like him; he is blameless and upright, a man who fears God and shuns evil." "Does Job fear God for nothing?" Satan replied. "Have you not put a hedge around him and his household and everything he has? You have blessed the work of his hands, so that his flocks and herds are spread throughout the land. But stretch out your hand and strike everything he has, and he will surely curse you to your face." The LORD said to Satan, "Very well, then, everything he has is in your power, but on the man himself do not lay a finger. Then Satan went out from the presence of the LORD" (Job 1:8-12)

Satan the accuser is given power to afflict, but is kept on a leash. All the evil he perpetrates upon humans and nature is under God's authority and power, limited by God. After Job's servants were murdered, his herds killed or stolen, and his children killed, his faith led him to see God's sovereign hand at work. When Job was told that while his sons and daughters were feasting and the wind caused the house to collapse on them and kill them he still worshiped God "and said: "Naked I came from my mother's womb, and naked I will depart. The LORD gave and the LORD has taken away; may the name of the LORD be praised" (Job 1:21).

The Second Test

> Then the LORD said to Satan, "Have you considered my servant Job? There is no one on earth like him; he is blameless and upright, a man who fears God and shuns evil. And he still maintains his integrity, though you incited me against him to ruin him without any reason." "Skin for skin!" Satan replied. "A man will give all he has for his own life. But stretch out your hand and strike his flesh and bones and he will surely curse you to your face." The LORD said to Satan, "Very well, then, he is in your hands; but you must spare his life." (Job 2:3-6)

As we read about the symptoms of Job's sickness we know that they included sores, the Hebrew translation is boils. These were described as painful and all over his body, from his head to his feet. He had a revolting appearance, became excessively thin and his breath was repulsive. He was in pain day and night. "His wife said to him, "Are you still maintaining your integrity? Curse God and die!""(Job 2:9). Satan used her just like he used Eve to tempt Adam. However, Job did not yield to that unspiritual advice, instead "He replied, "You are talking like a foolish woman. Shall we accept good from God, and not trouble?" In all this, Job did not sin in what he said" (Job 2:10).

Trouble and suffering are not merely punishment for sin. For God's people they may serve as trials, as in the case of Job. Trials, trouble, and suffering can produce discipline that culminates in spiritual gain, as in the case of Jesus.

Job endured what he did for a reason that, at the time, was beyond most human comprehension. After his friends sat and mourned with him for seven days, Job opened his mouth and cursed the day of his birth and his very existence as these had become an intolerable burden. All of these had formerly been a joy to him because of God's favor. He questioned why he could not have perished at birth or been stillborn, living in the grave he envisioned as a place of peace and rest. Even that seemed to be much better than his intolerable condition, in which he can find neither peace nor rest, only turmoil.

In response, his friends finally opened their mouths against him, making accusations that his illness and troubles were a result of some sort of sin in his life. His friend Bildad reasoned that Job and his family must be suffering as a result of sinfulness, and that Job should plead for mercy. Then God would restore him. Because of these severe accusations, Job asked Bildad how long he would torment and crush him with words. He asked Eliphaz to relent, to not be unjust, and to reconsider the things he said which had cast doubt on Job's integrity. What kind of friends would, in essence, kick Job when he was so down? Well-meaning, albeit and ignorant people, often do the same thing to us.

Job does not believe he is sinless, but he wishes to stand before God as one would go to court and stand before a judge to hear his charges. Job did not say that he was sinless, but innocent of any sin commensurate with his suffering. Since Job lived his life uprightly and blamelessly, feared God, and shunned evil, he imagined that God was angry with him—an innocent man—and began to wonder if God took delight in the wicked. We can say then that Job questioned God's motives and did not immediately acknowledge God's righteous judgment. Psalm 92:5-7 states, "How great are your works, LORD, how profound your thoughts! Senseless people do not know, fools do not understand, that though the wicked spring up like grass and all evildoers flourish, they will be forever destroyed." Psalm 92:12-17 states, "The righteous will flourish like a palm tree, they will grow like a cedar of Lebanon; planted in the house of the LORD, they will flourish in the courts of our God. They will still bear fruit in old age, they will stay fresh and green, proclaiming, "The LORD is upright; he is my Rock, and there is no wickedness in him.""

Some of the words Job spoke are a reminder that in times of severe suffering, people may say things that require a compassionate response of love and understanding. In love, God responded to Job. Job eventually repented and God forgave him. However, when Job was going through the test, he did not know that God had allowed Satan to crush him for a higher purpose. He continued to question God as if he were his adversary. He wanted to know why God, who created him, could all the while have planned to punish him even though he was not guilty of behavior that he believed warranted such suffering. Never considering that Satan was his oppressor, Job sought to understand why the all-powerful God would treat him so unjustly.

Job's friend, Zophar, along with his other two friends, claimed that Job suffered because of his sins. However, Zophar's failure to put himself in Job's place and condemning Job showed a lack of compassion. Job sincerely challenged what he perceived to be God's unjust actions, but had not mocked God or claimed himself to be pure. Though Bilded and Zophar were even more malicious, Eliphaz was guilty of cruel insinuation. If advice is helpful it is usually brief and encouraging, bringing hope, not lengthy, faultfinding and judgmental.

In summary of Job's situation, he said:

> "Though I cry, 'Violence!' I get no response; though I call for help, there is no justice. He has blocked my way so I cannot pass; he has shrouded my paths in darkness. He has stripped me of my honor and removed the crown from my head. He tears me down on every side till I am gone; he uproots my hope like a tree. His anger burns against me; he counts me among his enemies. His troops advance in force; they build a siege ramp against me and encamp around my tent. He has alienated my family from me; my acquaintances are completely estranged from me. My relatives have gone away; my closest friends have forgotten me. My guests and my female servants count me a stranger; they look on me as a stranger. I summon my servant, but he does not answer, though I beg him with my own mouth. My breath is offensive to my wife; I am loathsome to my own family. Even the little boys scorn me; when I appear, they ridicule me. All my intimate friends detest me; those I love have turned against me. I am nothing but skin and bones; I have escaped only by the skin of my teeth." (Job 19:7-20)

Job concluded that God was his enemy, though in fact, God was his friend who delighted in him.

Toward the end of Job's story, a fourth counselor spoke who had been listening to the dialogue and dispute, "So Elihu son of Barakel the Buzite said: "I am young in years, and you are old; that is why I was fearful, not daring to tell you what I know. I thought, 'Age should speak; advanced years should teach wisdom.' But it is the spirit in a person, the breath of the Almighty, that gives them understanding"'" (Job 32:6-8). He continued on, taking into consideration Job's emphasis on vindicating himself rather than God, viewing it as reprehensible.

Elihu believed that the inability of Job's friends to refute Job were tantamount to a condemnation of God. Elihu thought it was unjust and inconsistent for Job to expect vindication from God while implying that God did not care whether people were righteous. Elihu asserted that God was so far above human beings that there was really nothing they could do, good or bad, that would affect God's essential nature. He said: "If you sin, how does that affect him? If your sins are many, what does that do to him? If you are righteous, what do you give to him, or what does he receive from your hand? Your wickedness only affects a humans like yourself, and your righteousness only other people" (Job: 35:6-8). Elihu believed that Job needed an attitude correction; Job's complaints that God was silent were an offense to him. Elihu makes the point that the omniscient God of grace is good and just and not the author of evil and does not take his eyes off of the righteous.

> Why do you complain to him that he responds to no one's words? For God does speak—now one way, now another—though no one perceives it. In a dream, in a vision of the night, when deep sleep falls on people as they slumber in their beds, he may speak in their ears and terrify them with warnings, to turn them from wrongdoing and keep them from pride, to preserve them from the pit, their lives from perishing by the sword. Or someone may be chastened on a bed of pain with constant distress in their bones, so that their body finds food repulsive and their soul loathes the choicest meal. Their flesh wastes away to nothing, and their bones, once hidden, now stick out. They draw near to the pit and their life to the messengers of death. Yet if there is an angel at their side, a messenger, one out of a thousand, sent to tell them how to be upright, and he is gracious to that person and says to God,

'Spare them from going down to the pit; I have found a ransom for them—let their flesh be renewed like a child's; let them be restored as in the days of their youth' – then that person can pray to God and find favor with him, they will see God's face and shout for joy; he will restore them to full well-being. And they will go to others say, 'I have sinned, I have perverted what is right, but I did not get what I deserved. God has delivered me from going down to the pit, and I shall live to enjoy the light of life.' God does all these things to a person—twice, even three times—to turn them back from the pit, that the light of life may shine on them" (Job 33:13-30).

Elihu teaches that people do not receive the punishment that they deserve and it is out of love that God chastens them. In his frustration, Job came perilously close to charging God with wrongdoing. Elihu said that Job spoke without knowledge. How true that was, for Job did not know what was really going on, or what the conversation was between God and Satan. Our heavenly Father is full of mercy, far be it from him to do evil. I think that we can learn a great lesson here. We are not punished as we deserve because Jesus Christ took that punishment for us. We do not need to fear the punishment reserved for unrepentant sinners. We can trust that God has us and our circumstances in his hands.

Unaware of Satan's involvement, Elihu implies that God uses trouble to gain people's attention. God knows the spiritual needs of human beings and he knows how to redeem them. Our heavenly Father is patient with us. Often people suffer unnecessarily due to the hardness of their hearts and their refusal to yield to God, they will not cry out to him in their distress, or hear his voice in their suffering.

An important theme of the book of Job is that God's ways and thoughts are infinitely higher than ours. At the end of the book, God states that Job's complaints and rage against him were unjustified and proceeded from a limited understanding. He plied Job with rhetorical questions, to which Job had to plead ignorance in response. God said nothing about Job's suffering. Nor did he address Job's problem with divine justice. He gave Job neither a bill of indictment nor a verdict of innocence, though by implication, Job was vindicated. Later on, his vindication was directly affirmed by God through his restoration and abundant blessing of Job that exceeded all previous blessing he had received before his great season of suffering and tests. Despite Job's mistakes in word and attitude during his suffering, God commended Job but rebuked his friends who had counseled him.

Job spoke to God. His counselor friends spoke about God, but in their spiritual arrogance they claimed to possess knowledge they did not know. They presumed to know why Job was suffering. They were clueless of Satan's involvement. At the end of the book, Job's prayer for those who had abused him is a touching illustration of the high Christian virtue our Lord taught, "But I tell you, love your enemies and pray for those who persecute you" (Matthew 5:44). His prayer marked the turning point back to prosperity for him. The cosmic contest was over and Job was restored. There was no longer any reason for Job to experience suffering unless he was sinful and deserved it, which was not the case.

Our heavenly Father does not allow us to suffer for no reason, though the reason may be hidden in the mystery of his divine purposes. In this life we might never know why we suffer, but we must trust in him as the God who does only what is right—the God who is true to his word and promises.

Job finally sees that God is majestic and his purposes are just and supreme. Out of the awesome majesty of the thunderstorm, God spoke to Job and reminded him that the wisdom that directs the Creator's ways is beyond human understanding. Although we are created in God's image we should not assume that our wisdom could ever match his. Job made a futile attempt at justifying himself. The divine discourse brought Job to complete faith in God's wisdom and goodness, though he did not receive direct answers to his questions.

There are many times that we do not receive the answer that we want. We always receive the answer that we need.

Some Thoughts after Reading this Story

When pride comes, then comes disgrace, but with humility comes wisdom. (Proverbs 11:2)

Pride goes before destruction, a haughty spirit before a fall. (Proverbs 16:18)

Humble yourselves, therefore, under God's mighty hand, that he may lift you up in due time. Cast all your anxiety on him because he cares for you. Be alert and of sober mind. Your enemy the devil prowls around like a roaring lion looking for someone to devour. Resist him, standing firm in the faith, because you know that the family of believers throughout the world is undergoing the same kind of sufferings. And the God of all grace, who called you to his eternal glory in Christ, after you have suffered a little while, will himself restore you and make you strong, firm and steadfast. (1 Peter 5:6-10)

Submit yourselves, then, to God. Resist the devil, and he will flee from you. (James 4:7)

The Temptation of Jesus

Then Jesus was led by the Spirit into the wilderness to be tempted by the devil. After fasting forty days and forty nights, he was hungry. The tempter came to him and said, "If you are the Son of God, tell these stones to become bread." Jesus answered, "It is written: 'Man shall not live on bread alone, but on every word that comes from the mouth of God.'"

Then the devil took him to the holy city and had him stand on the highest point of the temple. "If you are the Son of God," he said, "throw yourself down. For it is written: "'He will command his angels concerning you, and they will lift you up in their hands, so that you will not strike your foot against a stone.'" Jesus answered him, "It is also written: 'Do not put the Lord your God to the test.'"

Again, the devil took him to a very high mountain and showed him all the kingdoms of the world and their splendor. "All this I will give you," he said, "if you will bow down and worship me." Jesus said to him, "Away from me, Satan! For it is written: 'Worship the Lord your God, and serve him only.'" Then the devil left him, and angels came and attended him. (Matthew 4:1-11)

How many of us would have proved ourselves like this? God does not have to prove he is God. Remember, his ways are higher than our ways. We do not have to prove we are children of God and co-heirs with Christ Jesus: God himself is our vindicator. Consider Job's futile attempt to justify himself.

With humility, Jesus beat pride, using only three sentences from the Word of God. There is power in the Word of God! God has a divine purpose for each of our lives. A key part of that purpose is to have faith, for without faith, it is impossible to please God. Jesus knew what his purpose was, and he practiced a faith that pleased God. He served God and man.

The Continued Temptation of Christ

"Now Jesus was going up to Jerusalem. On the way he took the twelve aside and said to them, "We are going up to Jerusalem, and the Son of Man will be delivered over to the chief priests and the teachers of the law. They will condemn him to death and will hand him over to the Gentiles to be mocked and flogged and crucified. On the third day he will be raised to life!"" (Matthew 20:17-19).

During the crucifixion of Jesus, "Those who passed by hurled insults at him, shaking their heads and saying, "You who are going to destroy the temple and build it in three days, save yourself! Come down from the cross if you are the Son of God!" In the same way the chief priests, the teachers of the law and the elders mocked him. "He saved others," they said, "but he can't save himself! He's the King of Israel! Let him come down now from the cross, and we will believe in him. He trusts in God. Let God rescue him now if he wants him, for he said, 'I am the Son of God'"" (Matthew 27:39-43). What if Jesus had come down from the cross? For our sake, it is good he did not, but he gave his life for us.

"Now faith is confidence in what we hope for and assurance about what we do not see" (Hebrews 11:1). "And without faith it is impossible to please God, because anyone who comes to him must believe that he exists and that he rewards those who earnestly seek him."(Hebrews 11:6). Jesus had faith in his Father and submitted to his will.

Jesus did not perform miracles for show, or use them like a bag of magic tricks. Prior to his crucifixion, some Pharisees and teachers of the law asked Jesus to perform a miraculous sign for them. "He answered, "A wicked and adulterous generation asks for a sign! But none will be given it except the sign of the prophet Jonah"" (Matthew 12:39). I highly doubt that the chief priests and teachers of the law were harlots, although some of them may have been. That is not what Jesus was referring to; his reference was to spiritual adultery. Those who worship God must worship him in spirit and in truth.

> Therefore, since we have been justified through faith, we have peace with God through our Lord Jesus Christ, through whom we have gained access by faith into this grace in which we now stand. And we boast in the hope of the glory of God. Not only so, but we also glory in our sufferings, because we know that

suffering produces perseverance; perseverance, character; and character, hope. And hope does not put us to shame, because God's love has been poured out into our hearts through the Holy Spirit, who has been given to us. You see, at just the right time, when we were still powerless, Christ died for the ungodly. Very rarely will anyone die for a righteous person, though for a good person someone might possibly dare to die. But God demonstrates his own love for us in this: While we were still sinners, Christ died for us. (Romans 5:1-8)

So we know that Jesus did the will of the Father and accomplished his mission, leaving us with an example to follow so that we too can be strong and overcome the world through him and with him as he abides in us. As was prophesied about him, so it was: "After he has suffered, he will see the light of life and be satisfied; by his knowledge my righteous servant will justify many, and he will bear their iniquities. Therefore I will give him a portion among the great, and he will divide the spoils with the strong, because he poured out his life unto death, and was numbered with the transgressors. For he bore the sin of many, and made intercession for the transgressors" (Isaiah 53:11-12).

He left us his example and these words: "Whoever does not take their cross and follow me is not worthy of me. Whoever finds their life will lose it, and whoever loses their life for my sake will find it" (Matthew 10:38-39). "Come to me, all you who are weary and burdened, and I will give you rest. Take my yoke upon you and learn from me, for I am gentle and humble in heart, and you will find rest for your souls. For my yoke is easy and my burden is light" (Matthew 11:28-30).

Through union with the exalted Christ, Christians have already been made beneficiaries of every spiritual blessing that belongs to and comes from the heavenly realm. Christ was raised from the dead by an extraordinary divine force or power, and that same force or power is at work in and through believers. However, we must put it into practice and live it out in our lives. Our human effort is inadequate, but God's power in us through the Holy Spirit is invincible.

By What Laws Are You Abiding?

The Pharisees and teachers of the law were just the religious leaders of that time, and obviously had nothing to do with following Jesus Christ. Are you a religious person or are you a Christian? There is a distinct difference. Jesus did not come to abolish the law, but to fulfill it. We are called to more than mere obedience to the law. For example, even the secular society we live in has laws we obey. There are more people who obey the law than who do not, in view of the number of those in prison being much smaller than the general population. However, here is some food for thought. In our secular society it is not illegal to gossip, lie, or commit adultery. Imagine if these were against the law. Our churches would be less full and our prisons overcrowded with convicted gossips, liars, and adulterers.

What if it were against the law to hate someone, be envious or jealous of them, or to covet what they have? What if it were illegal to use selfish ambition to get where you want to go? What if it were illegal to take advantage of others, trample on others' toes, cheat, deceive, or harm the welfare or character of another person? This happens all the time in the world's workplace, but is illegal in God's kingdom. Talk about sorting through the sheaves! There would be a lot of broken bundles to pull out the lawless ones. How empty many churches would be! We have too few jails to house all those who would break such laws.

Remember, God knows what is in your heart, no matter what kind of show you put on. That is why he called the religious leaders whitewashed tombs. They put on a good show, but their hearts were cold and dead toward God.

Christian character is produced by the Holy Spirit, not by the mere moral discipline of trying to live by the law. The indwelling of the Holy Spirit produces Christian virtues in the believer's life. However, we have to yield to this call. This is why many are called but few are chosen. In the parable of the wedding banquet, the king had the guest thrown out who was not wearing wedding clothes. I think of the imagery of a wedding as an expression of the intimate relationship between God and his people. Isaiah 61:10 says, "I delight greatly in the LORD; my soul rejoices in my God. For he has clothed me with garments of salvation and arrayed me in a robe of his righteousness, as a bridegroom adorns his head like a priest, and as a bride adorns herself with her jewels." We would not even think of attending a wedding banquet in improper attire, how much more so should we be properly clothed as the bride of Christ. "For many are invited, but few are chosen" (Matthew 22:14). "So I say, walk by the Spirit, and you will not gratify the desires of the flesh. For the flesh desires what is contrary to the Spirit and the Spirit what is contrary to the flesh. They are in conflict with each other, so that you are not to do whatever you want. But if you are led by the Spirit, you are not under law" (Galatians 5:16-18).

A Christian's contrary conduct is not due to ignorance of God's requirements but rather an act of one's self-will and rebellion. "If anyone, then, knows the good they ought to do and doesn't do it, it is sin for them" (James 4:17). When another Christian approves of such behavior, in so doing, he or she gives earthly, unspiritual, ungodly counsel, which is of the devil. When you operate in that realm of authority, you are in the jurisdiction of the authority you have placed yourself under: Satan. Taking all of this into consideration, you are being set up for destruction of some sort. Humans are not the real enemy, although they may be our opponents through which a spiritual evil can work. Human effort is inadequate to deal with such evil. However, through Christ, God has given us authority and power over all the vices of the enemy. Whatever happens; God can work it for the good of accomplishing his purpose.

As individual soldiers in God's army, we have to stand firm on his promises. As soldiers of Christ, we do not withstand assault by retaliating with brute force—definitely not by assaulting one another verbally, for when we do so, we lose the battle. Think of this: If soldiers are in a battle together and take their focus off it, both they and their fellow soldiers become easy prey for the enemy. As Christians, we are to be united in Christ, always remembering that the battle is spiritual and must be fought in God's strength (while depending on God and his Word, through prayer).

If you apply the Word of God in all that you do, you will not lay aside a piece of armor you need for protection. If you keep your focus on yourself and your own armor you will be successful in the battle. Let's look at the armor as listed in the book of Ephesians:

1. *The belt of truth.* Truth means conformity to fact. Fact is God's Word, which is truth. Conform means to act or be in compliance.

2. *The breastplate of righteousness.* A breastplate covers the heart, wherein lie our affections and emotions. Right means conforming to justice, law, or morality in accordance with fact.

3. *Feet fitted with the readiness that comes from the gospel of peace.* Ready means prepared or available for service or action.

4. *The shield of faith.* A shield is a means of defense. Faith is a confident belief in the truth.

5. *The helmet of salvation.* A helmet is designed to protect one's head and mind. Mind is a faculty of reason. Salvation means preservation or deliverance from evil or difficulty.

6. *The sword of the Spirit, which is the Word of God.* A sword is a weapon for cutting, death, and combat. The Spirit is the force of God who lives within us. The Word is something that is spoken.

7. *Pray in the Spirit on all occasions.* To pray is to address a petition to God. Spirit is the force of God who lives in us. Always

keep in mind that God is the perfect, omnipotent, omniscient originator and ruler that is in control of the universe.
8. *Be alert.* Alert means vigilantly attentive, watchful.
9. *Keep praying for the saints.* Keep petitioning God on behalf of other Christian brothers and sisters.

Put this all together and you can see how easy it has been for you to lay down a piece of armor and the many times this has allowed you to be wounded. Most of your battles are fought against the flesh. "The acts of the flesh are obvious: sexual immorality, impurity and debauchery; idolatry and witchcraft; hatred, discord, jealousy, fits of rage, selfish ambition, dissensions, factions and envy; drunkenness, orgies, and the like. I warn you, as I did before, that those who live like this will not inherit the kingdom of God" (Galatians 5:19-21).

> When you ask, you do not receive, because you ask with wrong motives, that you may spend what you get on your pleasures. You adulterous people, don't you know that friendship with the world means enmity against God? Therefore, anyone who chooses to be a friend of the world becomes an enemy of God. Or do you think Scripture says without reason that he jealously longs for the spirit he caused to dwell in us. But he gives us more grace. That is why Scripture says: "God opposes the proud but shows favor to the humble." Submit yourselves, then, to God. Resist the devil, and he will flee from you. (James 4:3-7)

Think about this; a divorce is permissible for a Christian who is involved with an immoral person, an adulterer. You know the grief that this causes. I imagine that God who jealously longs for us; the bride of Christ, feels that same sorrow when we are unfaithful.

Compromise and pride are spiritual adultery; they are impurities that will keep you out of the presence of God.

CHAPTER 7

KINGDOM LIVING

A kingdom is a territorial unit ruled by a king. It is the realm over which his sovereignty extends. God's kingdom is eternal. God is the Divine Creator who has revealed himself in creation. By a series of his royal creation decrees, he called into being the ordered world, the visible kingdom that those decrees continue to uphold and govern.

"In the beginning, God created the heavens and the earth. Now the earth was formless and empty, darkness was over the surface of the deep, and the Spirit of God was hovering over the waters. And God said, "Let there be light," and there was light. God saw that the light was good, and he separated the light from the darkness" (Genesis 1:1-3). The focus of this account in the book of Genesis, "formless and empty," gives structure to the rest of the chapter. God's *separating* and *gathering* on days 1-3 gave form. His *making* and *filling* on days 4-6 removed the emptiness. The described darkness and the waters complete the picture of a world awaiting God's light-giving, order-making, life-creating word. The majestic announcement that the mighty Spirit of God hovers over creation, anticipates God's creative words that follow.

The Spirit of God was *hovering*. The Holy Spirit was active in creation, and his creative power continues today. "In the beginning was the

Word, and the Word was with God, and the Word was God. He was with God in the beginning. Through him all things were made; without him nothing was made that has been made. In him was life, and that life was the light of all mankind. The light shines in the darkness, and the darkness has not overcome it" (John 1:1-5). This is a deliberate echo of Genesis 1:1: "In the beginning God created the heavens and the earth." This links God's salvation work through Jesus Christ with his first work; the creation of the world. The Word was with God and the Word was God. The Word was distinct from the Father and yet the Word was God.

"The Word became flesh and made his dwelling among us. We have seen his glory, the glory of the one and only Son, who came from the Father, full of grace and truth" (John 1:14). "He was in the world, and though the world was made through him, the world did not recognize him. He came to that which was his own, but his own did not receive him. Yet to all who did receive him, to those who believed in his name, he gave the right to become children of God—children born not of natural descent, nor of human decision or a husband's will, but born of God" (John 1:10-13). Therefore, in reading this and understanding these passages, as *children of God who are born of God,* we are related to Jesus Christ, the Son of God, and his Father is our Father. We are given the right to *become children*.

Understand this: We have the right to become. *Become means to grow or come to be, to be appropriate or suitable to*. This is a supernatural process that requires supernatural assistance. It cannot be accomplished in our own human effort. We need the counsel of our heavenly Father. He sends us the Holy Spirit to lead, guide, and direct us into all truth. All children need to be taught. Good behavior is learned through discipline.

Moses and the Presence and Glory of God

Consider all that God told Moses to do. He spoke with Moses. Moses did as he was told. God miraculously made provision, miracle after miracle. In Exodus 33:13, Moses prayed: "If you are pleased with me, teach me your ways so I may know you and continue to find favor with you. Remember that this nation is your people." Moses made intercession for the people and God answered him. "The LORD replied, "My Presence will go with you, and I will give you rest"" (Exodus 33:14).

God's favor was in his actions on behalf of his people, despite their rebellious ways. As Moses prayed in Exodus 34:9, ""Lord," he said, if I have found favor in your eyes, then let the Lord go with us. Although this is a stiff-necked people, forgive our wickedness and our sin, and take us as your inheritance." "Then the LORD said: "I am making a covenant with you. Before all your people I will do wonders never before done in any nation in all the world. The people you live among will see how awesome is the work that I, the LORD, will do for you. Obey what I command you today. I will drive out before you the Amorites, Canaanites, Hittites, Perizzites, Hivites and Jebusites. Be careful not to make a treaty with those who live in the land where you are going, or they will be a snare among you" (Exodus 34:10-12). God said he would drive them out, but to not make a treaty with them (a treaty is an agreement).

Keep in mind; these civilizations of people God was going to drive out were lewd in their religious practices. For example, El, the head of the Canaanite pantheon, had three wives who were patronesses of sex and war, but they were also his sisters. He was the bloody tyrant who dethroned his own father, murdered his favorite son, and decapitated his own daughter. According to religious literature of that time, unearthed at Ras Shamra (ancient Ugarit in North Syria), the Ugaritic poems present him as a lustful, morbid character. El (Abu Shania, or "father bull") was the progenitor of the gods. Baal, the widely revered Canaanite deity who was also given to moral abandon, was the son of El, and dominated the Canaanite pantheon. The Canaanite cults were utterly immoral, characterized by self-indulgence and corruption. They were dangerous spiritual contaminants that thoroughly justified the divine command to destroy their devotees. There are dangerous spiritual contaminants in the world with which we must be careful not to make a treaty (an agreement) or compromise with.

Just as the Israelites were impatient with Moses and constructed a golden idol (a calf) to worship instead of God, we too have to be careful not to be impatient with God and construct idols in place of him. Do not compromise the application of the Word of God in your life, no matter what the situation.

Moses asked God to show him his glory, "And the LORD said, "I will cause all my goodness to pass in front of you, and I will proclaim my name, the LORD, in your presence. I will have mercy on whom I will have mercy, and I will have compassion on whom I will have compassion. But," he said, "you cannot see my face, for no one may see me and live"" (Exodus 33:19-20).

From the fullness of his grace we have all received one blessing after another, just like the Israelites. As the law was given through Moses, grace and truth came through Jesus Christ. "No one has ever seen God, but the one and only Son, who is himself God and is in closest relationship with the Father, has made him known" (John 1:18).

Therefore, God has made himself known to us through Jesus Christ. Since we know God as our heavenly Father through Christ, we also know that he desires to lead, guide, direct, and provide for us. Jesus said, "The thief comes only to steal and kill and destroy; I have come that they may have life, and have it to the full" (John 10:10). We know that Satan (the thief) wants to steal God's blessings from us, but he is unable to do so, unless we make a treaty (an agreement of compromise) with him.

Unity with the Trinity

After Jesus prayed for his disciples, he prayed for all believers:

> "My prayer is not for them alone. I pray also for those who will believe in me through their message, that all of them may be one, Father, just as you are in me and I am in you. May they also be in us so that the world may believe that you have sent me. I have given them the glory that you gave me, that they

may be one as we are one—I in them and you in me—so that they may be brought to complete unity. Then the world will know that you sent me and have loved them even as you have loved me. Father, I want those you have given me to be with me where I am, and to see my glory, the glory you have given me because you loved me before the creation of the world. Righteous Father, though the world does not know you, I know you, and they know that you have sent me. I have made you known to them, and will continue to make you known in order that the love you have for me may be in them and that I myself may be in them." (John 17:20-26)

God is love. Jesus' prayer was that his love would be in us. The unity of God with us should have an effect on outsiders and convince them of the mission of Christ. In essence, Jesus' prayer can be considered as a rebuke of the types of divisions among believers. Believers are to be characterized by *humility and service,* just as Christ was, so that God's glory will rest on them. Jesus prayed to his Father, that believers would be one, just as he and his Father are one. Again, the Lord emphasized the importance of unity among his followers, and again, the standard is the unity of the Father and Son, "I in them and you in me."

There are two kinds of indwelling referred to here: that of the Son in believers, and that of the Father in the Son. It is because of the reality of the Father in the Son that the Son can be in believers, thereby making us children of God. When the love of the Father and Jesus Christ is in us it is evident and on display. This unity has an evangelistic aim. It is connected, with Jesus' mission and the love God has for people and Christ. We did not know God directly and personally, but we know that out of his love and mercy for us, God sent Christ that we might know him as our heavenly Father. Recognizing God in Christ's mission is eye opening to the world. To not know Christ is to be ignorant of the Father. This is why Jesus called the Pharisees blind guides. In knowing Christ we all have a calling and that is to be his disciples. We also all have a vision to seek and save the lost. As we walk in a kingdom lifestyle we will bear fruit, people will see Jesus through us.

> "If you remain in me and my words remain in you, ask whatever you wish, and it will be done for you. This is to my Father's glory, that you bear much fruit, showing yourselves to be my disciples. As the Father has loved me, so have I loved you. Now remain in my love. If you keep my commands, you will remain in my love, just as I have kept my Father's commands and remain in his love. I have told you this so that my joy may be in you and that your joy may be complete. My command is this: Love each other as I have loved you. Greater love has no one than this: to lay down one's life for one's friends. You are my friends if you do what I command. I no longer call you servants, because a servant does not know his master's business. Instead, I have called you friends, for everything that I learned from my Father I have made known to you. You did not choose me, but I chose you and appointed you so that you might go and bear fruit—fruit that will last – and so whatever you ask in my name the Father will give you. This is my command: Love each other.
>
> If the world hates you, keep in mind that it hated me first. If you belonged to the world, it would love you as its own. As it is, you do not belong to the world, but I have chosen you out of the world. That is why the world hates you. Remember what I told you: 'A servant is not greater than his master.' If they persecuted me, they will persecute you also. If they obeyed my teaching, they will obey yours also." (John 15:7-20)

A Righteous Status

We still have to do the right thing, even in the midst of persecution. The world hated the disciples as followers of Christ. Because Christians do not belong to the world, persecution from the world is inevitable. The basic reason for persecution is the world's ignorance of and rejection of the Father and the Son, Jesus Christ. Keep in mind that it is the Spirit within you they are rejecting. Jesus said he would send the Counselor. "When the Advocate comes, whom I will send to you from the Father – the Spirit of truth who goes out from the Father – he will testify about me. And you also must testify, for you have been with me from the beginning" (John 15:26-27). Jesus was speaking to the disciples. They were to go out and make more disciples. This is the Great Commission. As Christians, we are to testify. Believers are responsible to bear their own testimony to and of Christ in the power of the Spirit.

The Holy Spirit is our counselor; he is with us to help us. Jesus described the work that he would do. "When he comes, he will prove the world to be in the wrong about sin and righteousness and judgment:" (John 16:8). The work that the New Testament normally speaks of the Holy Spirit doing in the world is his work in believers. Unbelief and sin blind people from seeing themselves as sinners. The work that the Spirit does is convict people, so that they can see themselves as they truly are. Only the Holy Spirit can reveal to a person that their good works do not gain a righteous status before God. This is where religious belief can be so blinding. When Jesus died, the curtain of the temple was torn in two, from top to bottom. The curtain that separated the holy place from the most holy place, and it's tearing, signified Christ making it possible for believers to go directly into God's presence.

Jesus said that the Holy Spirit proves the world to be wrong in regard to judgment because the *prince of this world now stands condemned*. Jesus was referring to the defeat of Satan. Christ already defeated Satan and his final judgment is inevitable. A prince is a hereditary ruler, the ruler of a principality. A principle is first, highest, or foremost in importance in rank, worth, or degree. Consider what is important to worldly people; things of that kingdom. Satan is the prince of their world, the ruler over the things of the world. Since he is condemned as their ruler then what would they fall under but condemnation?

This is where he wants people to be, in the dark. Satan suffers defeat when we resist him.

Pride, material abundance, and self-control are three things with which Satan tested Jesus Christ while he was in the world. How much more so will he tempt us? Pride is a stumbling block that is in place before a fall. "Those who want to get rich fall into temptation and a trap and into many foolish and harmful desires that plunge people into ruin and destruction. For the love of money is a root of all kinds of evil" (1 Timothy 6:9-10). The lack of self-control can branch into any area of your life to cause you to create an idol of almost anything that overcomes you. We are to seek first the kingdom of God and his righteousness, and all other things that we need will be added to us. God did it for the Israelites and God will do it for you, too. This will happen when you get your focus off of things and onto God's agenda and headed on the path that he has mapped out for you.

Jesus *bore our iniquities*. Through repentance and acceptance of him, he can take the idols away (if you give them up). Think about what that means. That he *bore* them means he accepted and became accountable for them. *Iniquity* includes wickedness, sinfulness, grossly immoral acts, injustice, and more. He bore those things for us so that we can be forgiven of them and they are not held to our account.

When you have an idol before God you are subjecting yourself to the government of that idol and no longer to God's government. When someone falls subject to the government of any other government than that of God the Father, it usually means trouble is on the horizon and in the making. There are often residual effects of living under the jurisdiction of that government. The upcoming short story (Fine Dining in a War Zone) will exemplify this principle.

Satan seeks to rob, steal the blessings of a kingdom lifestyle, bring destruction, destroy and kill. The sooner sin is dealt with, the better for the individual involved. Satan does not want people to know this. Sin is ugly and destructive. It causes division and separates people, churches, and homes. It is harmful and hurtful. (Jesus bore sin on the cross. It was an ugly sight. The nails hurt and he was grossly disfigured by what he endured for us.) Sin causes lewd behavior, factions, and dissension. Sin separates you from God. Once separated, you are out of his realm of jurisdiction (living in the sinful world through participation) and subject to the ruler of that kingdom, the ruler of the world (Satan). I find it hard to believe that anyone would actually want to live under the jurisdiction of the one described in the book of Revelation as a dragon. Our Loving Heavenly Father wants us to know the truth because it will set us free.

"When you were dead in your sins and in the uncircumcision of your flesh, God made you alive with Christ. He forgave us all our sins, having canceled the charge of our legal indebtedness, which stood against us and condemned us; he has taken it away, nailing it to the cross. And having disarmed the powers and authorities, he made a public spectacle of them, triumphing over them by the cross" (Colossians 2:13-15).

In Matthew 27:46, Jesus Christ quotes the words of Psalm 22:1 as he waits to die on the cross: "About three in the afternoon Jesus cried out in a loud voice, "Eli, Eli, lema sabachthani?" (which means "My God, my God, why have you forsaken me?"). Jesus was at that point in the world where he was subject to the government of the world. All of those who were in authority there (or so they thought), killed him. This was done intentionally for us. He intentionally subjected himself to the worldly powers. God the Father orchestrated this entire situation for a higher purpose. They did kill the physical body of Christ, however, only by his submission.

There is one more thing to take into consideration. Do you remember when the mockers said that if Jesus were truly God, he should come down from the cross? Satan would have loved to have seen that, for it would have defeated the entire purpose of Christ's mission in the world. This is how we too are supposed to live, crucifying the flesh and bringing it under submission to the Spirit of God so that we will accomplish our mission. We do not need to prove who we are to the world. Jesus rose from the dead just as he said he would. God had a bigger picture and plan in mind. Christians are part of that plan. We too will have a glorified body at the appointed time.

Fine Dining in a War Zone

When Satan tempted Jesus, "Jesus answered, "It is written: 'Man shall not live on bread alone, but on every word that comes from the mouth of God'" (Matthew 4:4). This scripture had new significance to a woman when she was put to the test on her newly acquired job. This story gives an awesome example of the passage in Psalm 23:5, "You prepare a table before me in the presence of my enemies." It became relative to the spiritual feast she became a partaker of during her employment at this job. When you eat, you physically grow and gain strength. The same principle applies to spiritual growth as God's words, precepts, laws, and principles are put into action in one's life.

After being victimized by circumstances arising from choices she made, and coming off a road that nearly led to her literal physical and mental destruction, this woman's story begins with her vow to put God first in her life from that point forward. After escaping the situation, she could look back and see the protection of her Heavenly Father, who in the midst of her wrong decision heard her cries and plea for help. Yet she was unaware she still had a lot more to learn as she desired to walk with Christ and do his work.

She had to start over again. After a bad choice left her with nothing but her farm and her life, she was immediately blessed with two part-time jobs, though she worked seven days a week and had no benefits. At times, she lived rather haphazardly, still having to overcome some bad habits she had acquired and a worldly lifestyle that would land her in the devil's jurisdiction from time to time.

While assisting a friend with his crop, she fell off a hay wagon, cracking two ribs and a tooth. She then wacked her head in the same place two times, causing a fracture that added more medical bills.

The medical bills from these injuries took years for her to pay. As a result of these incidents, she decided to look for a job with medical and other benefits, just in case of more mishaps, as the last two had been so costly.

Once again, she called on God to get her out of the trouble she had gotten into. Each day, she grew in grace and drew closer to her Heavenly Father, giving up the baggage she had been carrying with her from her previous excursions and lifestyle. Ever the faithful Father, God answered (though his answer did not turn out to be what she expected). God orchestrated her circumstances, which turned out to be for her own good, resulting in spiritual growth. The whole plan of answer was for a greater good that, at the time, she was unable to foresee.

Her food service experience led her to apply for a job as a manager of a local school cafeteria. One morning, she was praying for God to move her to another position where she would have benefits. She heard him say, "I will move you, today." When she got home from work, there was a message for her to call the school to set up an interview. After two panel interviews and a considerable amount of time, she was offered a new job. She was excited that the food service director, a professing Christian who held office in a local church, was going to be her boss (and the boss's secretary was a professing Christian as well).

Opposition

After she was hired, she found out that the director had recommended that her position be reclassified and her pay cut. Another Christian who worked there told her that the reason for her second interview was that the food service director actually had someone else in mind for the job. She thought that changing the interview panel might sway the vote against her. An individual who was asked to be on the second interview panel informed her of this. This person also shared being asked by the food service director to write a letter of recommendation for the other applicant. In spite of the letter, the woman gained more votes from the interview panel because she was much more qualified for the job. (This person begged the woman not to repeat any of this, out of fear of being fired.) The food service director's plan did not work. God's plan prevailed.

The first point of this story is that, when God speaks, he is faithful to keep his word. The second point is, no man can manipulate or stop what God has set out to do. The third point is that your life is a witness and a testimony to God's provision for his children.

Persecution

The woman gave thanks to God for her new job and set off to work, intent on doing her job as one working for God. She was determined to be the best witness and testimony she could be, and to make the most of every opportunity. And opportunity she had, though not the type she expected. The witness was more one of perseverance through trials she underwent. She experienced great opposition, slander, false accusations, and mocking from employee's she had to oversee as part of her job. The food service director did everything within the power of the position to make her job as difficult as possible, leaving her to figure out on her own the policies, procedures, and paperwork she needed to fill out.

This did not go unnoticed by an officer worker who, at one time, held her position. This worker went to great lengths to assist her in filling out the necessary paperwork. She was greatly encouraged by a born-again Christian janitor who spoke to her just about every day. Even one of the children wrote her sweet notes, encouraging her to not let their meanness upset her. She was encouraged by the little children she loved and looked forward to serving each day. In these and many other ways, God was with her throughout that trying time.

From time to time, one employee who professed to be a born-again Christian tried to come to her defense, but to no avail. Another one of her employees, also a professing Christian, continually stirred up trouble in the group. The rest of her employees were fearful of this person due to the relationship this person had with the food service director. Though they knew the persecution was going on, they were fearful of attempting to do anything about it.

The director would soon retire. In spite of her grief, through tears, the woman was determined to just hang in there, thinking that when the director retired, things would certainly get better. On many days, when she prayed, she was led to read Psalm 22. Each morning she was led to read that psalm, it would prepare her for the events that would transpire that day. It encouraged her to know that the psalm King David wrote was as real to him as it applied to Christ. Like her, they felt abandoned. Yet God never left them alone and heard their cry. She believed God would never leave her, and that he would surely hear her cry. She also knew that somehow, some way, God would work it all together for her good. So despite the opposition and direct harassment she suffered, she was submissive and did her work as one working for God himself, knowing he placed her there for a reason beyond her current comprehension.

When it came time for interviews of candidates to replace the director, the director's secretary, a professing Christian who seemed very nice, called her and told her to apply for the job. The secretary said that even though the director had told her the job was hers, the secretary was not interested in it. The woman also received a call from a person who worked in the human resources department, encouraging her to apply for the job. Though she was hesitant to apply, she did, but did not get the job. The secretary had also applied, and she got the job. The woman was not sure why the secretary had lied to her, but she was sure of one thing: things would get worse.

Perseverance in Persecution

The new director (the former secretary) grew extremely hateful and hostile toward her. On top of this, her friend the janitor retired, and the person who took his position was friends with the crowd.

When some teachers told her stories about a shooting that had taken place in the school, years ago, she immediately missed her friend, the retired janitor, as he used to open up the building each morning at the same time that she came in to open up the cafeteria. After hearing of the shooting, she was fearful of opening up the cafeteria without him being there. One day, she found screws dumped under her tires. On another occasion, someone had driven a spike into the side of one of her car's tires, causing a flat. She started to park her car in the front of the building where the teachers parked and was questioned by her boss about it. *Hmmm, why would that even concern her?*, she wondered. This caused her to be fearful for her life.

Going to work became increasingly like going to hell. She was in fear and tears almost every day—it was becoming more than she could bear. She spoke with the individual in administration who had previously informed her of the former director's plans to keep her from getting her job in the beginning, as she also knew what was going on and what she was going through. In tears, she told the person she did not know how much more she could endure. She also would not involve this person (for she knew of the manipulative scheme the former director had employed to try to prevent her from getting her job, something the woman had kept in strict confidence). A witness like this who knew what had transpired and what was going on, if called forward to give an account, quite possibly could have helped her make her case against the administration and get her promised pay and a better working environment. However, there were just too many others who were aligned against her, and others so fearful of losing their jobs if they stood up for her that they turned a blind eye to her predicament. Her supporter in administration said she was sorry she had voted for her to get the job, after seeing the hostility and grief she was enduring. The only option suggested was to complain to the superintendent of the school system.

Deepening her predicament, her boss was a professing Christian she had seen in her own church, so she was uncertain it would be a good decision to take it any further. She decided to take it to God himself.

She prayed and asked God what she should do. God's word not to retaliate was confirmed to her. When one of the school's administrative staff came to speak with her after finding out about the situation, she said she did not want to discuss any of it. She prayed and asked God to help her forgive the whole bunch and to GET HER OUT! Once again, her request was granted! She landed a job closer to home that paid three times what she had made at the school. Best of all, she no longer had to go to work in fear!

What lessons can one learn from this story?

1. God always answers prayer.
2. When God speaks, he is faithful to keep his word.
3. When you are happy, praise God.
4. No man can stop what God has set out to do.
5. Do not betray a confidence.
6. Since Peter denied Christ three times after being with him and (knowing who he was), why even expect behavior from other people to be any different?
7. Practice forgiveness.
8. How to pray for those who mistreat you.
9. Your life is a witness and testimony to God's provision for you as his child.
10. Always thank God for his provision.
11. You will be blessed when you persevere through trials.
12. You will be blessed when you are mocked.
13. Not everyone who claims to be a Christian lives like one.
14. Two wrongs do not make a right. So always make the right decision and you will be blessed.
15. People have a tendency to fear the created more than the Creator.
16. Bad company corrupts good character.
17. It takes a strong person to stand for righteousness.

18. You can be strong in the Lord and in his mighty power.
19. God will never allow you to go through more than you can endure.
20. God gives grace to the humble.
21. Submit to rulers and authorities God has ordained.
22. Seek and pursue peace as far as it concerns you.
23. It is better to suffer for doing good than for doing evil.
24. Do not repay evil for evil.
25. Keep your conscience clear so that those who speak maliciously against your good behavior in Christ will be ashamed of their slander.
26. Fear not, for God is with you, even to the ends of the earth.
27. God has not given us a spirit of fear, but of love, power, and a sound mind.
28. When you are in trouble, pray.
29. Blessed are the poor in spirit.
30. The poor will eat and be satisfied.
31. After you have suffered a little while, God himself will restore you and make you strong, firm, and steadfast.

In Psalm 22:3-5, David goes on to say: "Yet you are enthroned as the Holy One; you are the one Israel praises. In you our ancestors put their trust; they trusted and you delivered them. To you they cried out and were saved; in you they trusted and were not put to shame." In Psalm 22:23-28, he says:

> You who fear the LORD, praise him! All you descendants of Jacob, honor him! For he has not despised or scorned the suffering of the afflicted one; he has not hidden his face from him but has listened to his cry for help. From you comes the theme of my praise in the great assembly; before those who fear you will I fulfill my vows. The poor will eat and be satisfied;

they who seek the LORD will praise him—may your hearts live forever! All the ends of the earth will remember and turn to the LORD, and all the families of the nations will bow down before him, for dominion belongs to the LORD and he rules over the nations.

Seeking and praising the Lord gets his attention. Those who seek him find him. When you find him, praise is much more appropriate than grumbling.

"And we know that in all things God works for the good of those who love him, who have been called according to his purpose. For those God foreknew he also predestined to be conformed to the image of his Son, that he might be the firstborn among many brothers and sisters" (Romans 8:28-29). "What, then, shall we say in response to these things? If God is for us, who can be against us? He who did not spare his own Son, but gave him up for us all—how will he not also, along with him graciously give us all things?" (Romans 8:31-32). God knew what the woman in the story needed. She needed all those lessons that came out of the story. They were gifts that could not be purchased with gold or silver. They were gifts that only God could give to her—gifts of eternal value. These gifts enabled her to live a kingdom lifestyle governed by the Prince of Peace, Jesus Christ.

Two Kingdom's Collide

A prince is a ruler of a principality. If that ruler is condemned, those he rules over in that principality and jurisdiction are condemned as well. A principality is a territory. Satan is the prince of this world, and is condemned to death. I believe that as we grow spiritually that the light of the life of Christ within us transforms the darkness around us.

"Jesus said, "My kingdom is not of this world. If it were, my servants would fight to prevent my arrest by the Jewish leaders. But now my kingdom is from another place"" (John 18:36). "When Jesus spoke again to the people, he said: "I am the light of the world. Whoever follows me will never walk in darkness, but will have the light of life"" (John 8:12).

"In the beginning was the Word, and the Word was with God, and the Word was God. He was with God in the beginning. Through him all things were made; without him nothing was made that has been made. In him was life, and that life was the light of all mankind. The light shines in the darkness, but the darkness has not overcome it" (John 1:1-5).

Judgment: "This is the verdict: Light has come into the world, but people loved darkness instead of light because their deeds were evil. Everyone who does evil hates the light, and will not come into the light for fear that their deeds will be exposed. But whoever lives by the truth comes into the light, so that it may be seen plainly that what they have done has been done in the sight of God" (John 3:19-21).

Possession of eternal life involves both human faith and divine appointment. Jesus has chosen us out of the world. The world is darkness, and in Christ there is no darkness. Therefore, if you are in Christ, you are a reflection of that light and there is no darkness in you. Jesus was the Messianic servant, and as Christians, we are those who continue that servant's mission. Though God created the destroyer to work havoc, the Word says: "no weapon forged against you will prevail, and you will refute every tongue that accuses you. This is the heritage of the servants of the LORD, and this is their vindication from me,' declares the LORD" (Isaiah 54:17).

"The night is nearly over; the day is almost here. So let us put aside the deeds of darkness and put on the armor of light" (Romans 13:12). This is a clear example of the nearness of the end times. Do you hear the call?

As true Christians, you are in the world but not of the world, the principality governed by its prince. As a true believer, you are in Christ,

Christ is in God, and God is not in the world. His kingdom is not of this world.

God came to the world in the man, Jesus Christ (who was a ransom for us), who is the Word. God was in him and he is in us. The Word became flesh and dwelt among us. So, "Take the helmet of salvation and the sword of the Spirit, which is the word of God" (Ephesians 6:17). This is why Jesus said his kingdom was not of this world, which is why his servants did not fight to prevent his arrest—the battle is not carnal.

Keep in mind: "In the beginning God created the heavens and earth. Now the earth was formless and empty, darkness was over the surface of the deep, and the Spirit of God was hovering over the waters" (Genesis 1:1-2). God created everything and is in control of everything; however, he gave us each a free will. It is not automatic, we must wholeheartedly allow God to form us in his way and fill us with his light. We have to empty ourselves of what we have in essence built on our own beliefs. Solomon stood before the alter of God "and said: " LORD, the God of Israel, there is no God like you in heaven above or on earth below—you who keep your covenant of love with your servants who continue wholeheartedly in your way" (1 Kings 8:23). He went on to say: "But will God really dwell on earth? The heavens, even the highest heaven, cannot contain you. How much less this temple I have built!" (1 Kings 8:27).

God has to build us. He cannot be contained in our flesh, just as the temple could not contain God. On our own, without the provision Christ made for us, we are not able to maintain a relationship with God. God met with the Israelites through the priests in the temple. Now God gives us the instructions and the Counselor (Advocate), the Holy Spirit, to lead and guide us to our meeting place with our Heavenly Father. His Spirit dwells within us. All we have to do is be submissive and obedient. He will see us to completion. Philippians 1:6 says, "being confident of this, that he who began a good work in you will carry it on to completion until the day of Jesus Christ."

The Greatest Command

"Love the Lord your God with all your heart and with all your soul and with all your mind and with all your strength" (Mark 12:30). Real love requires growth and maturity, knowledge, strength, depth of insight into God's will, practical discernment, and sensitivity, with understanding. Christians are to discern, approve, and put into practice what is morally and ethically superior. Christians are to be filled with the fruit of righteousness. There is no room for mixture. The goal of the Christian life is to be pure and blameless, without any mixture of evil, thereby, not being open to censoring of the world, condemnation of Satan, or of conscience because of moral or spiritual failure. Light and darkness do not mix. Where there is light, darkness is overcome!

"If you suffer, it should not be as a murderer or thief or any other kind of criminal, or even as a meddler. However, if you suffer as a Christian, do not be ashamed, but praise God that you bear that name. For it is time for judgment to begin with the Gods household; and if it begins with us, what will the outcome be for those who do not obey the gospel of God?" (1 Peter 4:15-17). I would rather be under scrutiny now, while I have the time to change.

The world judges according to human standards, from a darkened understanding. They do not understand why God's people no longer follow their sinful way of life. The world misunderstood Christ. They will misunderstand you as a follower of his. A wicked and evil person will be abusive, even to the death of a true believer. Godly living alone can bring persecution. "In fact, everyone who wants to live a godly life in Christ Jesus will be persecuted, while evil doers and impostors will go from bad to worse, deceiving and being deceived" (2 Timothy 3:12-13).

The godlessness of the last days is obvious. "But mark this: There will be terrible times in the last days. People will be lovers of themselves, lovers of money, boastful, proud, abusive, disobedient to their parents, ungrateful, unholy, without love, unforgiving, slanderous, without self-control, brutal, not lovers of the good, treacherous, rash, conceited, lovers of pleasure rather than lovers of God—having a form of godliness but denying its power. Have nothing to do with such people" (2 Timothy 3:1-5). God will deal with them. On the flip side, do not be deceived: bad company corrupts good character, so be careful of evil associations. There is a clear line between being a witness and having a relationship that is something other than being a witness. This, too, can become a trap.

Light and darkness do not mix, though light is seen in darkness. We live in a dark world.

The description above is congruent with the types of worldly people who persecute true Christians. If we know this is their character description, why should we expect anything else from them? They are darkened in their understanding. We are called to be light. We are also an extension of Christ's love.

Therefore: "Do your best to present yourself to God as one approved, a worker who does not need to be ashamed and who correctly handles the word of truth. Avoid godless chatter, because those who indulge in it will become more and more ungodly" (2 Timothy 2:15-16).

So watch who you associate with most closely. We have to give an account of our actions as well as for our words spoken. Therefore, we need to be self-controlled and our words must be those of light, truth, peace, and joy. Words we speak must be gentle, kind, and faithful, with patience, and always express godly love. Knowing the condition of society and the immoral behavior of people, we also must be careful not to let our love grow cold, thereby losing that key piece of the armor of God: our feet fitted with the readiness that comes from the gospel of peace. We must not alienate ourselves from those who are perishing out of fear. Our job is to tell them the good news. Remember, perfect love casts out fear. We cannot give up on them. After all, God did not give up on us.

> Flee the evil desires of youth, and pursue righteousness, faith, love and peace, along with those who call on the Lord out of a pure heart. Don't have anything to do with foolish and stupid arguments, because you know they produce quarrels. And the Lord's servant must not be quarrelsome but must be kind to everyone, able to teach, not resentful. Opponents must be gently instructed, in the hope that God will grant them repentance leading them to knowledge of the truth, and that they will come to their senses and escape from the trap of the devil, who has taken them captive to do his will. (2 Timothy 2:22-26)

To walk in the truth of 2 Timothy 2:22-26 is to bear fruit. Forgiveness is key to bearing fruit. We need to forgive even churchgoing, professing Christian persecutors, who behave no differently than the Pharisees and Sadducees of Christ's time. Pay no mind to them, except to pray for them. God will deal with them. Keep the following words of Jesus in mind:

> "A good tree cannot bear bad fruit, and a bad tree cannot bear good fruit. Every tree that does not bear good fruit is cut down and thrown into the fire. Thus, by their fruit you will recognize them. Not everyone who says to me 'Lord, Lord,' will enter the kingdom of heaven, but only he who does the will of my Father who is in heaven. Many will say to me on that day, 'Lord, Lord, did we not prophesy in your name and in your name drive out demons and perform many miracles?' Then I will tell them plainly, 'I never knew you. Away from me, you evildoers!'" (Matthew 7:18-23)

At the Great White Throne Judgment, Jesus will be well aware of those who forget to add that they were crafty, gossips, slanderers, unforgiving, self-seeking, and prideful (to name a few). Pay them no mind.

Jesus said:

> "I am the true vine, and my Father is the gardener. He cuts off every branch in me that bears no fruit, while every branch that does bear fruit he prunes so that it will be even more fruitful. You are already clean because of the word I have spoken to you. Remain in me, as I also remain in you. No branch can bear fruit by itself; it must remain in the vine. Neither can you bear fruit unless you remain in me." (John 15:1-4)

So think of this the next time you are in a hurtful situation, or something is taken from you. Remember that quite possibly; what was taken from you could have been dead wood pruned away for your fruitful benefit. This is what Jesus meant by calling us to bear fruit: "But to you who are listening I say: Love your enemies, do good to those who hate you, bless those who curse you, pray for those who mistreat you. If someone slaps you on one cheek, turn to them the other also. If someone takes your coat, do not withhold your shirt from them" (Luke 6:27-29).

"Here is a trustworthy saying: If we died with him, we will also live with him; If we endure, we will also reign with him. If we disown him, he will also disown us; if we are faithless, he remains faithful, for he cannot disown himself" (2 Timothy 2:11-13). Do not be discouraged. Never give up. Ask and you will receive assistance. Treat others how you would like to be treated. Keep in mind that one may be acting in ignorance, as you once have, so have mercy on them as your Heavenly Father has mercy on you. Remember to act on what you know to be good, as we align our actions with faith we please God.

When the disciples asked Jesus about the parables that he spoke, "He told them, 'The secret of the kingdom of God has been given to you. But to those on the outside everything is said in parables so that, "they may be ever seeing but never perceiving, and ever hearing but never understanding; otherwise they might turn and be forgiven!"'" (Mark 4:11-12).

If you ever feel inadequate, just remember it is not you who can do anything for the kingdom; it is the kingdom within you that is given freely to you, the working of God and the Holy Spirit who equip you to follow in Jesus Christ's footsteps. The kingdom of God had seemingly insignificant beginnings, introduced by the despised and rejected Jesus and his twelve unimpressive disciples. However, a day will come when the whole world will see its true greatness and power. This is our glorious hope.

The Father's House

Jesus said, "My Father's house has many rooms; if that were not so, would I have told you that I am going there to prepare a place for you?" (John 14:2). He also said, "For I tell you that unless your righteousness surpasses that of the Pharisees and the teachers of the law, you will certainly not enter the kingdom of heaven" (Matthew 5:20).

Jesus did not speak against observing all the requirements of observing the law, nor the teaching of the same. He spoke against hypocritical legalism. Such legalism was not genuine in that all of the details of the law were being kept. It was deceitful and lacking depth, an empty pretense. The laws were kept externally to gain merit before God and to be seen by men, while breaking them inwardly. In essence, they were following the letter of the law while ignoring its true spirit. Jesus repudiated the Pharisees' interpretation of the law and their view of works as external righteousness. Jesus spoke of a righteousness that comes not by human works, but only through faith in him and his redemptive work. He asked: "Don't you believe that I am in the Father and that the Father is in me? The words I say to you I do not speak on my own authority. Rather, it is the Father, living in me, who is doing his work" (John 14:10).

Jesus' teaching was not of human origin. His words were his father's words. The two are one. There was an inseparable connection between his words and his work. Saving faith is trust in a person, but it must have factual content. Faith includes believing that Jesus is one with the Father. He said, "Very truly I tell you, whoever believes in me will do the works I have been doing, and they will do even greater things than these, because I am going to the Father. And I will do whatever you ask in my name, so that the Father may be glorified in the Son. You may ask me for anything in my name, and I will do it" (John 14:12-14). It is time for the church to do great things. Are you ready?

John the Baptist came as a forerunner of Christ. "In those days John the Baptist came, preaching in the wilderness of Judea and saying, "Repent, for the kingdom of heaven has come near" (Matthew 3:2). Repentance is not merely a change of one's mind or an act of contrition, but involves a radical change in one's lifestyle. True repentance is a whole life turn around and involves forsaking sin for good, and turning or returning to God. The prodigal son left the pig pen and returned home. It was there he received blessing. The *kingdom of heaven/kingdom of God* as Jesus taught is recounted in the Gospel's as the *reign of God* that is brought to us through *Jesus Christ*. It includes the establishment of God's rule in the hearts and lives of his people. This is fulfillment of Jeremiah's prophesy about the coming new covenant. As part of the new covenant God said that he would put his law in our hearts. The kingdom of God through the reign of Jesus Christ, overcame all of the forces of evil. Jesus (The Lamb of God) came to remove all of the consequences of sin from the world. He was the final and ultimate sacrifice defeating death. We have access to the power of a kingdom lifestyle and to overcome all that diminishes life and are enabled to live abundantly. Living in kingdom lifestyle is life in a new order of righteousness and peace that has been ordained by God.

The idea of God's kingdom is central to Jesus' teaching. This is why he taught:

> "Therefore I tell you, do not worry about your life, what you will eat or drink; or about your body, what you will wear. Is not

life more important than food, and the body more important than clothes? Look at the birds of the air; they do not sow or reap or store away in barns, and yet your heavenly Father feeds them. Are you not much more valuable than they? Can anyone of you by worrying add a single hour to his life? And why do you worry about clothes? See how the flowers of the field grow. They do not labor or spin. Yet I tell you that not even Solomon in all his splendor was dressed like one of these. If that is how God clothes the grass of the field, which is here today and tomorrow is thrown into the fire, will he not much more clothe you – you of little faith? So do not worry, saying, 'What shall we eat?' or 'What shall we drink?' or 'What shall we wear?' For the pagans run after all these things, and your heavenly Father knows that you need them. But seek first his kingdom and his righteousness, and all these things will be given to you as well." (Matthew 6:25-33)

Shadrach, Meshach, and Abednego refused to serve Nebuchadnezzar's gods. They told him that they did not need to defend themselves, and that their God could deliver them. Even if he did not, they continued, they would not bow down to Nebuchadnezzar's gods. So Nebuchadnezzar had them bound and thrown into a blazing furnace. He was amazed to see four unharmed and unbound men walking around in the fire. They were a witness to the king because of their faith and trust in God and their obedience to his word. "Then Nebuchadnezzar said, 'Praise be to the God of Shadrach, Meshach and Abednego, who has sent his angel and rescued his servants! They trusted in him and defied the king's command and were willing to give up their lives rather than serve or worship any god except their own God'" (Daniel 3:28). "King Nebuchadnezzar, to the nations and peoples of every language, who live in all the earth: May you prosper greatly! It is my pleasure to tell you about the miraculous signs and wonders that the Most High God has performed for me. How great are his signs, how mighty his wonders! His kingdom is an eternal kingdom; his dominion endures from generation to generation" (Daniel 4:1-3).

What God did for Shadrach, Meshach and Abednego, was not only noticed by others, but God was praised for his mighty works. Just knowing that someone sincerely appreciates what I have done for them makes me want to do more. When someone expresses gratitude and I see their joy it makes me happy. When someone compliments me on a project that I have completed, it really makes me feel great that they noticed. Our Heavenly Father has created us in his image. I truly believe that he feels emotion just like we do. (Read Psalm 92.)

When we recognize, honor, and thank our Heavenly Father for what he does for us it brings him joy. When we testify about his mighty works and the miracles that he has performed on our behalf he knows that we hold him highly esteemed. When we give God the Father, the Son and the Holy Spirit the credit that they deserve, he will move mightily on our behalf and display his glory. We are assured that life is abundant and peaceful in the kingdom of God.

CHAPTER 8

ACCEPTING THE CALL

Many are called, but few are chosen. The invitation must be accepted, and then acted upon by appropriate conduct. Proper behavior is evidence of being chosen.

"The kingdom of heaven is like a king who prepared a wedding banquet for his son. He sent his servants to those who had been invited to the banquet to tell them to come, but they refused to come" (Matthew 22:2-3).

Commenting on feasting in the kingdom of God, "Jesus replied: A certain man was preparing a great banquet and invited many guests. At the time of the banquet he sent his servant to tell those who had been invited, 'Come, for everything is now ready.' But they all alike began to make excuses. The first said, 'I have just bought a field, and I must go and see it. Please excuse me.' Another said, 'I have just bought five yoke of oxen, and I'm on my way to try them out. Please excuse me.' Still another said, 'I just got married so I can't come'" (Luke 14:16-20). Acceptance of the invitation is not the end: attendance is required to be a partaker. To *attend* means to apply or direct oneself. Acceptance or acknowledgment that Jesus is Christ is just the beginning. Even Satan accepts the fact that Jesus is the Christ. You may very well accept Jesus Christ, but then you have to work out your salvation by practical application of his kingdom principles in your everyday life.

Jesus said: "Make every effort to enter through the narrow door, because many, I tell you, will try to enter and will not be able to. Once the owner of the house gets up and closes the door, you will stand outside knocking and pleading, 'Sir, open the door for us.' But he will answer, 'I don't know you or where you come from.' Then you will say, 'We ate and drank with you, and you taught in our streets.' But he will reply, 'I don't know you or where you come from. Away from me, all you evildoers!'" (Luke 13:24-27).

In spite of very large crowds that came to hear Jesus' preaching and be healed, there were only a few followers who were loyal. Think about the fact that churches are full of people every week. What percentage of those in attendance do you think are loyal followers of Jesus Christ?

> "Listen then to what the parable of the sower means: When anyone hears the message about the kingdom and does not understand it, the evil one comes and snatches away what was sown in their heart. This is the seed sown along the path. The seed falling on rocky ground refers to someone who hears the word and at once receives it with joy. But since they have no root, they last only a short time. When trouble or persecution comes because of the word, they quickly fall away. The seed falling among the thorns refers to someone who hears the word, but the worries of this life and the deceitfulness of wealth choke the word, making it unfruitful. But the seed falling on good soil refers to someone who hears the word and understands it. This is the one who produces a crop, yielding a hundred, sixty or thirty times what was sown." (Matthew 13:18-23)

When reading these passages, I think of the thousands of people who attend churches at their convenience. Maybe they pay their tithe out of obligation, or maybe not. Maybe they just give him what is left over (if there is anything left that they haven't indulged on themselves). I think about people who add God to their life, rather than give their life to him as their Lord. There are multitudes of people who call themselves Christians; they are ever hearing and never understanding the truth of the teachings of Jesus Christ. These people have a form of godliness but deny the power of God. They seek to be blessed and entertained, to watch the show that other church people put on. Some of them even participate in the functions and fellowships. They have a commitment that only expects blessings. Some of these people are very religious and in positions of leadership in their church. Though they faithfully serve the church or the community, they live and act in a manner inconsistent with true godliness. Though they perform good works (supposedly for God), their hearts are far from him. They are judgmental, gloating and their prayers are merely manipulative, much like witchcraft, not answered by God but heard by Satan. We need to remain alert at all times, so that these deceptions do not overcome us. We are in a real spiritual battle.

Serving God and allowing Christ to be the Lord of your life is not merely an outward action. It is not just what you do, but how you act all the time, consistently, in all circumstances. It is how you think.

"He told them still another parable: "The kingdom of heaven is like yeast that a woman took and mixed into about sixty pounds of flour until it worked all through the dough"" (Matthew 13:33). As yeast permeates a batch of dough, so the kingdom of heaven spreads through a person's life. Yeast may also signify the growth of the kingdom by the inner working of the Holy Spirit—an inward rising to outward growth. God has given us the opportunity to live a kingdom lifestyle within his kingdom. He wants to impart the gift of the Holy Spirit upon us, to lead, guide, and direct us. All that we can give to him is our life in submission to his will for us.

God has called us. Listen to the call of Jeremiah: "The word of the LORD came to me, saying, "Before I formed you in the womb I knew you, before you were born I set you apart; I appointed you as a prophet to the nations"'" (Jeremiah 1:4-5). The Hebrew verb used here is translated *chosen*. In verse six, Jeremiah said, "'Alas, Sovereign LORD," I said, "I do not know how to speak; I am too young""' (Jeremiah 1:6). Despite Jeremiah's view of himself, God did with him what Jeremiah did not think he was capable of doing. He went on to be a prophet to the nations because *God chose him* to do so. He also acknowledged the call and kept and fulfilled his appointment.

God created him	God created you
Set him apart	Set you apart
Appointed him	Appointed you
Equipped him	Equipped you

"You are a chosen people, a royal priesthood, a holy nation, God's special possession, that you may declare the praises of him who called you out of darkness into his wonderful light" (1 Peter 2:9). The key words here are: chosen, royal, priesthood, and holy. "For those God foreknew he also predestined to be conformed to the image of his Son, that he might be the firstborn among many brothers and sisters. And those he predestined, he also called; those he called, he also justified; those he justified, he also glorified" (Romans 8:29-30). God knows that we are incapable of accomplishing royal behavior without training. Fulfilling the character, vocation, and office of a priest, and that being holy as our Heavenly Father is holy, is not in our inherent nature. It is impossible to achieve this type of behavior without renewal that comes only through having the mind of Christ and the counsel of the Holy Spirit.

Jesus said: "Very truly I tell you, whoever believes in me will do the works I have been doing, and they will do even greater things than these, because I am going to the Father" (John 14:12). He went on to say in John 14:15-17: "If you love me, keep my commands. And I will ask the Father, and he will give you another advocate to help you and be with you forever—the Spirit of truth. The world cannot accept him, because it neither sees him nor knows him. But you know him, for he lives with you and will be in you." In 2 Corinthians 3:17-18 we read: "Now the Lord is the Spirit, and where the Spirit of the Lord is, there is freedom. And we, who with unveiled faces contemplate the Lord's glory, are being transformed into his image with ever-increasing glory, which comes from the Lord, who is the Spirit." In John 17:22, Jesus said, "I have given them the glory that you gave me, that they may be one as we are one."

As believers, our lives are to be characterized by humility and service, just as Christ was. It is then that God's glory rests on us and becomes evident in our life. The Lord emphasized the importance of unity. Part of Jesus' prayer was that we would be in him and as a result, be united with the Father: "I in them and you in me—so that they be brought to complete unity. Then the world will know that you sent me and have loved them even as you have loved me" (John 17:23). The standard of unity is the Father and the Son. The Son listened to the Father and was submissive to his will and guidance. Above all else, he acted in love.

Do you think you can put yourself in his sandals? None of these things are hard to accomplish, for the gifts of God are free and Christ already paid the price and made the way for us. He told us: "Take my yoke upon you and learn from me, for I am gentle and humble in heart, and in you will find rest for your souls. For my yoke is easy and my burden is light" (Matthew 11:29)

Jesus said: "Ask and it will be given to you; seek and you will find; knock and the door will be opened to you. For everyone who asks receives; the one who seeks finds; and to the one who knocks, the door will be opened" (Matthew 7:7-8). If you seek the right things—the things of the kingdom—you will receive them. When you receive a gift from God you can then give it away, for gifts are intended to be given. Paul said, "I became a servant of this gospel by the gift of God's grace given me through the working of his power" (Ephesians 3:7). Our Heavenly Father can do far beyond what we could ever even think or imagine.

We must be careful to remember that all the needs represented in our prayers and petitions to God on behalf of others are met by God, not us. He imparts his gifts to us and others for his glory, not ours. If we begin to think or brag about the positive results of our prayers for ourselves or others, we do not bring glory to God, but feed our pride. This is why some once prosperous ministries have fallen apart. You can be sure that pride comes before a fall. Remember, God disperses the gifts. We are only there to deliver them as he gives them to us to give away.

Listen to what Jesus said in Matthew 7:21-23: "Not everyone who says to me, 'Lord, Lord', will enter the kingdom of heaven, but only the one who does the will of my Father who is in heaven. Many will say to me on that day, 'Lord, Lord, did we not prophesy in your name and in your name drive out demons and perform many miracles?' Then I will tell them plainly, 'I never knew you. Away from me, you evildoers!'" We certainly do not want to be in that line!

Today, if you hear God's voice speaking to you, be of good courage and act upon it while it is still today. Jesus said, "Therefore everyone who hears these words of mine and puts them into practice is like a wise man who built his house on the rock" (Matthew 7:24). "We must pay the most careful attention, therefore, to what we have heard, so that we do not drift away. For since the message spoken by angels was binding, and every violation and disobedience received its just punishment, how shall we escape if we ignore so great a salvation? This salvation, which was first announced by the Lord, was confirmed to us by those who heard him. God also testified to it by signs, wonders and various miracles, and gifts of the Holy Spirit distributed according to his will" (Hebrews 2:1-4).

The gospel is greater than the law. If disregard for the law brought certain punishment, disregard for the gospel will bring even greater punishment. The supernatural manifestations of the Spirit and gifts are distributed to us as God sees fit. However, we have to be submissive to the Spirit in order for him to work through us. I pray that God will revive us and that we will boldly testify to such a great salvation. We have received a great gift, and God gave it to us freely. I pray that we will freely give it to all who cross our path and allow the Holy Spirit to lead, guide, and direct us wherever our feet lead us. I pray that he will powerfully confirm the truth of his Word.

> There are different kinds of gifts, but the same Spirit distributes them. There are different kinds of service, but the same Lord. There are different kinds of working, but in all of them and in everyone it is the same God at work. Now to each one the manifestation of the Spirit is given for the common good. To one there is given through the Spirit a message of wisdom, to another a message of knowledge by means of the same Spirit, to another faith by the same Spirit, to another gifts of healing by that one Spirit, to another miraculous powers, to another prophecy, to another distinguishing between spirits, to another speaking in different kinds of tongues, and to still another the interpretation of tongues. All these are the work of one and the same Spirit, and he distributes them to each one, just as he determines. (1 Corinthians 12:4-11)

Manifestations of the Spirit can only exist where the Spirit is received. Through the same Spirit he works all things in all men together for a common purpose, to glorify Jesus Christ who loves us so much that he sent the Holy Spirit to us as a gift and seal of his love. "Peter replied, "Repent and be baptized in the name of Jesus Christ for the forgiveness of your sins. And you will receive the gift of the Holy Spirit. The promise is for you and your children and for all who are far off—for all whom the Lord our God will call" (Acts 2:38-39).

If you have heard God's call on your life, you have access to the gift he wants you to have; a gift that will enable you to be successful in your walk of life that leads to the goal of eternal life. Union with Christ gives us permission to accept the gift of the Holy Spirit so that our lives may overflow with the fruit of the Spirit. The Holy Spirit is a gift that helps us in our weakness. "In the same way, the Spirit helps us in our weakness.

> We do not know what we ought to pray for, but the Spirit himself intercedes for us through wordless groans. And he who searches our hearts knows the mind of the Spirit, because the Spirit intercedes for God's people in accordance with the will of God.
>
> And we know that in all things God works for the good of those who love him, who have been called according to his purpose. For those God foreknew he also predestined to be conformed to the image of his Son, that he might be the firstborn among many brothers and sisters. And those he predestined, he also called; those he called, he also justified; those he justified, he also glorified. What, then, shall we say in response to these things? If God is for us, who can be against us? He who did not spare his own Son, but gave him up for us all—how will he not also, along with him, graciously give us all things? (Romans 8:26-32)

Gifts that God has given to all of us are those we choose to accept through the Holy Spirit. As a believer, you are entitled to make the choice of the type of life you live.

Life in the Spirit	**Life in the Flesh**
1) Love—Godly affection, selfless devotion	1) Debauchery—Extreme indulgence of ones sensual pleasures, seduction from morals
2) Joy—Rejoicing, happiness, delight of mind	2) Idolatry—Ascription of divine power to any created thing, excessive devotion
3) Peace—Freedom from disturbance, tranquility	3) Fits of rage—Furious uncontrolled anger

4) Patience—Endurance, consistency, forbearance	4) Hatred—Abhor, ill will, loathsome
5) Kindness—Sympathetic, benevolent, generous	5) Discord—Disagree, conflict, inharmonious
6) Goodness—Pleasant, beneficial for wellbeing	6) Jealousy—Resentful interest, envious
7) Faithfulness—Maintaining allegiance, trust	7) Witchcraft—Sorcery, use of magical arts to harm, heal, manipulate, curse and spite
8) Gentleness—Affable, not harsh, not violent	8) Selfish Ambition—Desire to succeed at any length to gain a particular objective
9) Self Control—Control of emotions, desires and actions	9) Dissensions—Disagreements with strife
	10) Factions—A Group of people forming a contention that is often contemptuous and rive, or a rival group, within a larger group
	11) Envy—Discontent and ill will because of another's advantage, coveting, jealousy
	12) Drunkenness—Intoxicated to the point of impairment of mental and physical faculties, habitually overcome
	13) Orgies—Licentious merrymaking, disregard for accepted rules, morally unrestrained

How Does Your Lifestyle Add Up?

Are you intentionally giving up the gifts of God for the things of the world and the sinful nature? How much grief God must feel when we do not accept his good gifts. What are you doing with what God has given you? Jesus expounded on this in one of his parables on what the kingdom of heaven will be like:

> "Again, it will be like a man going on a journey, who called his servants and entrusted his wealth to them. To one he gave five bags of gold, to another two bags, and to another one bag, each according to his ability. Then he went on his journey. The man who had received the five bags of gold went at once and put his money to work and gained five bags more. So also, the one with the two bags of gold gained two more. But the man who had received the one bag went off, dug a hole in the ground and hid his master's money. After a long time the master of those servants returned and settled accounts with them. The man who had received the five bags of gold brought the other five. 'Master,' he said, 'you entrusted me with five bags of gold. See, I have gained five more.' His master replied, 'Well done, good and faithful servant! You have been faithful with a few things; I will put you in charge of many things. Come and share your master's happiness!' The man with the two bags of gold also came. 'Master,' he said, 'you entrusted me with two bags of gold; see, I have gained two more.' His master replied, 'Well done, good and faithful servant! You have been faithful with a few things; I will put you in charge of many things. Come and share your master's happiness!' Then the man who had received the one bag of gold came. 'Master,' he said, 'I knew that you are a hard man, harvesting where you have not sown and gathering where you have not scattered seed. So I was afraid and went out and hid your gold in the ground. See, here is what belongs to you.' His master replied, 'You wicked, lazy servant! So you

knew that I harvest where I have not sown and gather where I have not scattered seed? Well then, you should have put my money on deposit with the bankers, so that when I returned I would have received it back with interest. So take the bag of gold from him and give it to the one who has ten bags. For everyone who has will be given more, and they will have an abundance. Whoever does not have, even what they have will be taken from them. And throw that worthless servant outside, into the darkness, where there will be weeping and gnashing of teeth.'" (Matthew 25:14-30)

The present-day use of a talent is an ability or gift intended to be given away. The main point of being ready for Christ involves more than playing it safe and doing little or nothing. It demands the kind of service that produces results. God does not have to use us; he chooses to use us. He called, appointed, and equipped us. If we do not respond, it will not stop his work; he will just get someone else to do it and quite possibly bless them with a gift that was ours for the asking or receiving.

What are some of the reasons we do not respond to God's offer of free gifts? Why do we not accept the gifts God has endowed us with for the purpose of giving them away and, thus, miss out on multiplying them? Pride, fear, and greed are among the top reasons. Think about what Jesus did with his gifts; he gave them away, even though the recipients were not worthy.

God is still available today, and is willing to give us a second chance. It is his desire to revive us. Oh, how we need revival! We are so blessed! Why then do we not act like it? (After all, *act* comes from the word *action*.) What are your acts like? Go back and review life in the Spirit versus the lifestyle of the flesh. Make the change now, while it is still today! Today, if you hear his voice, do not harden your heart. "now that you have tasted that the Lord is good" (1Peter 2:3). What type of live ought we to be living? How about living a life that is worthy of our calling?

"When you ask, you do not receive because you ask with wrong motives, that you may spend what you get on your pleasures. You adulterous people, don't you know that friendship with the world means enmity against God? Therefore, anyone who chooses to be a friend of the world becomes an enemy of God" (James 4:3-4). Since God is love, he wants us to give love away in turn; we are to walk in love. If we truly walk in love, in our own lifestyle, we will walk in and speak the truth. What is the truth? God's Word! It is the truth that sets people free, not compromise. Even if they do not want to hear the truth, it is to their benefit to hear it, for they may accept it, turn from their way, and be saved. Furthermore, it is a requirement that we not cause anyone to stumble. There is no room for compromise in God's kingdom.

In Exodus 20:4, God said, "You shall not make for yourself an image in the form of anything in heaven above or on earth beneath or in the waters below. You shall not bow down to them or worship them; for I, the LORD your God, am a jealous God punishing the children for the sin of the parents to the third and fourth generation of those who hate me, but showing love to a thousand generations of those who love me and keep my commandments." God has exclusive rights to possess and claim our love, total allegiance, and implicit trust in him. We should be expressing that trust in faithful and obedient service.

> Therefore, my dear friends, flee from idolatry. I speak to sensible people; judge for yourselves what I say. Is not the cup of thanksgiving for which we give thanks a participation in the blood of Christ? And is not the bread that we break a participation in the body of Christ? Because there is one loaf, we, who are many, are one body, for we all share the one loaf. Consider the people of Israel: Do not those who eat the sacrifices participate in the altar? Do I mean then that food sacrificed to an idol is anything, or that an idol is anything? No, but the sacrifices of pagans are offered to demons, not to God, and I do not want you to be participants with demons. You cannot drink the

cup of the Lord and the cup of demons too; you cannot have a part in both the Lord's Table and the table of demons. Are we trying to arouse the Lord's jealousy? Are we stronger than he? (1 Corinthians 10:14-22)

The exercise of one's freedom is to be governed by whether or not it will bring glory to God.

Evil Gains Entrance

I saw an evil spirit of infliction standing off to the side of the church. He was watching and waiting for an opportunity. I saw compromise shake his hand. A deal was made, he gained his opportunity, and he was given authority to inflict harm. Compromise is a settlement in which each side gives up some demands or makes concessions; an adjustment of opposing principles. A principle is that which is first in rank, authority, or importance. To *inflict means to give or cause pain, to strike, or to impose punishment upon.*

Shaking hands with the demon was an agreement, thereby giving up a principle that was of first importance and authority. Compromise gives authority to the one with whom the compromise is made, making him first in rank. So then, part of the deal was accepting infliction. Any deal with a demon can never be a good one, yet people do it all the time, and then wonder why they are going through what they are going through, and why things are happening the way they are happening. When you compromise with Satan, you give him the authority to rob, steal, and destroy. Satan is very happy when Christians compromise. It is an open door for him to move in for the kill.

America is a good place to live, but what about its godliness? Misused favor can turn into failure very rapidly. Freedom can turn into captivity. Captivity can steal blessing. What was once a land of the free and home of the brave can change. Without repentance, we are on the brink of some dark days ahead. We cannot continue to compromise and expect to be blessed by God. *You cannot drink of both cups.*

Consider that we battle not against flesh and blood but the rulers and principalities of this dark world. The battle is spiritual and must be fought in God's strength, in dependence upon the Word and on God, through prayer. We need to be courageous and prayerfully consider what we condone.

> Finally, be strong in the Lord and in his mighty power. Put on the full armor of God, so that you can take your stand against the devil's schemes. For our struggle is not against flesh and blood, but against the rulers, against the authorities, against the powers of this dark world and against the spiritual forces of evil in the heavenly realms. Therefore put on the full armor of God, so that when the day of evil comes, you may be able to stand your ground, and after you have done everything to stand. Stand firm then, with the belt of truth buckled around your waist, with the breastplate of righteousness in place, and with your feet fitted with the readiness that comes from the gospel of peace. In addition to all this, take up the shield of faith, with which you can extinguish all the flaming arrows of the evil one. Take the helmet of salvation and the sword of the Spirit, which is the word of God. And pray in the Spirit on all occasions with all kinds of prayers and requests. With this in mind, be alert and always keep on praying for all the Lord's people. (Ephesians 6:10-18)

STAND

Let Satan huff, let Satan puff and let Satan blow
For in Christ we know
Where we stand, and that God has us by the hand,
That our God is ultimately in control
We need to let fear roll
Right on by and out of the way
On God's decrees and principles and in his Word we stay,

Making the right choices while it is still today,
For God has given us this land upon which we stand
It is our choice which way we go.
It is our choice to wander to and fro.
Or to move on in and to begin
To lay claim to that which already belongs to us
No matter how much the world makes a fuss.
For we already know the fate that lies ahead
Our eternal promised new homestead.
If we do what we know to be right
We know that is our plight.
Since perfect love casts out fear
Let's boldly serve God who holds us so dear
That he gave his only son
And in us then the work has begun,
Let us see it through to the end
And not let compromise God's ways bend
To appease the crowd
No matter how loud,
We are still led by that quiet still voice
The Holy Spirit who helps us to make the right choice.
(Kathleen Poulton, August 6, 2014)

Compromise out of fear of loss is a trick of the devil—thinking that it is okay this time to condone a little evil, for if I do not I may suffer some loss. It does not matter what the loss may be; count the real cost. Losing any kind of support, financial or from people, is not worth losing God's support, and possibly giving up one's place in eternity. I know that scripture says that he is faithful even when we are not, but it also says; "If anyone, then, knows the good they ought to do and doesn't do it, it is sin for them" (James 4:17). There is a difference between an ignorant action and willful actions. We do not know at what hour or day Christ will return, but we should live like it may be today. "As obedient children, do not conform to the evil desires you had when you lived in ignorance" (1 Peter 1:14).

"Pride goes before destruction, a haughty spirit before a fall. Better to be lowly in spirit along with the oppressed than to share plunder with the proud" (Proverbs 16:18-19). "To fear the Lord is to hate evil; I hate pride and arrogance, evil behavior and perverse speech" (Proverbs 8:13).

I saw another spirit that entered the church. It was an adulterous and proud mocker. It entered in to discredit our accountability. I saw it prancing to and fro haughtily, flaunting itself. I saw yet another spirit of pride had gained entrance into the church. Adultery and rampant pride are active within the walls of the church. As a result of this crippled leadership has taken a place in the church. Where this happens there is music but not worship. "Therefore, I urge you, brothers and sisters, in view of God's mercy, to offer your bodies as a living sacrifice, holy and pleasing to God—this is your true and proper worship" (Romans 12:1). As I read this scripture I think about how the animals presented as a sacrifice had to be without defect. "Do not bring anything with a defect, because it will not be accepted on your behalf" (Leviticus 22:20). In John 4:23, Jesus said, "Yet a time is coming and has now come when the true worshipers will worship the Father in the Spirit and in truth, for they are the kind of worshipers the Father seeks." Just think of all the "defects" in the people who attend church, sing, and make music with the same mouth and body they have offered up in an unholy manner all week long.

When I saw these spirits, I thought about the letters to the churches in the book of Revelation. These letters are an example for us. As I read through them, the passages jumped off the page to me as a clear warning for the church.

1. To the church at Pergamum that held to the teaching of Balaam, which deceived believers into compromise with worldliness.
2. To the church at Thyatira that tolerated Jezebel, this undermined loyalty to God by promoting tolerance toward pagan practices.

3. To the church at Sardis, a city of great wealth and fame. Its deeds were incomplete and they were disobedient to the Word and unrepentant.
4. To the church at Laodicea, because they were lukewarm (neither hot nor cold), God warned them he was about to spit them out of his mouth.

All of these can apply to America. They are creeping into the church. "Those whom I love I rebuke and discipline. So be earnest, and repent. Here I am! I stand at the door and knock. If anyone hears my voice and opens the door, I will come in and eat with that person, and they with me" (Revelation 3:19-20). I believe that God is trying to get our attention.

Persevere

In closing, I would like to say that I have been through some rough times; times of hurt, sorrow, and abuse by others. I have been through hard times financially and seasons of sickness. I have been used, taken advantage of, deserted, abandoned, mocked, ridiculed, and slandered. Psalm 22 was a great encouragement to me during several seasons in my life when I could relate to the crucifixion of Jesus. I was able to endure circumstances and events I was going through knowing that if I truly wanted to be a follower of Christ, I had to deny myself, pick up my cross, and follow him daily. I had to deny myself by bringing my flesh into submission to the application of the Word of God for all details of my emotional and physical reactions to what I was enduring. This is a difficult training process, but well worth the results.

Paul said, "Do you not know that in a race all the runners run, but only one gets the prize? Run in such a way as to get the prize. Everyone who competes in the games goes into strict training. They do it to get a crown that will not last, but we do it to get a crown that will last forever. Therefore I do not run like someone running aimlessly; I do not fight like a boxer beating the air. No, I strike a blow to my body and make it my slave so that after I have preached to others, I myself will not be disqualified for the prize" (1 Corinthians 9:24-27). "Blessed is the one who perseveres under trial because, having stood the test, that person will receive the crown of life that the Lord has promised to those who love him" (James 1:12).

Knowing that we must love the Lord with all our heart, mind, and soul tells me that we have to bring our heart, mind, and soul into submission to the Word of God and properly apply it in every area of life, in all situations and circumstances. "Consider it pure joy, my brothers and sisters, whenever you face trials of many kinds, because you know that the testing of your faith produces perseverance. Let perseverance finish its work so that you may be mature and complete, not lacking anything" (James 1:2-4). "What good is it, my brothers and sisters, if someone claims to have faith but has no deeds? Can such faith save them?" (James 2:14). When God says he will provide for you, he means he will do just that! When you truly love your neighbor as yourself, you treat him as you would want him to treat you. When you walk in love, you will stop cheating, lying, conniving, and stepping on toes. You will no longer slander or gossip to gain something at the expense of another. Then, God will provide for you.

You cheat yourself out of God's provision and lie to yourself when you think God's Word is not true and choose not to apply it in your life. God's Word is applicable to every situation in our lives. God is true to his Word; his Word is truth. There is no wickedness in God. God is no respecter of persons; however, respect is something we earn. We cannot earn anything on our own and give it to God. It is only through Christ and putting into action his teaching in our live, that we can gain the attention of God. God then holds us highly esteemed and whatever we ask, He will give to us. We will receive because we ask with right motives. We will give and it will be given unto us in bountiful measure. A complete blessing will be poured into our lives, for with the measure we use—our life action—it will be measured to us. Our deeds will then be good and of kingdom value. These deeds are faith in practical action.

I have written Psalm 22 below, with some notes, numbered *(Note 1)* to *(Note 7)* throughout the psalm that corresponds with the numbers listed below the psalm.

> My God, my God, why have you forsaken me? Why are you so far from saving me, so far from my cries of anguish? My God, I cry out by day, but you do not answer, by night, but I find no rest. Yet you are enthroned as the Holy One; you are the one Israel praises. In you our ancestors put their trust; they trusted and you delivered them. To you they cried out and were saved; in you they trusted and were not put to shame. But I am a worm and not a man, scorned by everyone, despised by the people. All who see me mock me; they hurl insults, shaking their heads: "He trusts in the LORD," they say, "let the LORD rescue him. Let him deliver him, since he delights in him." Yet you brought me out of the womb; you made me trust in you even at my mother's breast. From birth I was cast on you; from my mother's womb you have been my God." (Psalm 22:1-10) *(Note 1)*

> Do not be far from me, for trouble is near and there is no one to help. Many bulls surround me; strong bulls of Bashan encircle me. Roaring lions that tear their prey open their mouths wide against me. I am poured out like water, and all my bones are out of joint. My heart has turned to wax; it has melted within me. My mouth is dried up like a potsherd, and my tongue sticks to the roof of my mouth; you lay me in the dust of death. Dogs surround me; a pack of villains encircles me, they pierce my hands and my feet. All my bones are on display; people stare and gloat over me. They divide my clothes among them and cast lots for my garment. (Psalm 22:11-18) *(Note 2)*

> But you, LORD, do not be far from me. You are my strength; come quickly to help me. (Psalm 22:19) *(Note 3)* Deliver me from the sword, my precious life from the power of the dogs. (Psalm 22:20) *(Note 4)*

Rescue me from the mouth of the lions; save me from the horns of the wild oxen. I will declare your name to my people; in the assembly I will praise you. You who fear the LORD, praise him! All you descendants of Jacob, honor him! Revere him, all you descendents of Israel! (Psalm 22:21-23) *(Note 5)*

For he has not despised or scorned the suffering of the afflicted one; he has not hidden his face from him but has listened to his cry for help. From you comes the theme of my praise in the great assembly; before those who fear you I will fulfill my vows. (Psalm 22:24-25) *(Note 6)*

The poor will eat and be satisfied; those who seek the LORD will praise him—may your hearts live forever! All the ends of the earth will remember and turn to the LORD, and all the families of the nations will bow down before him, for dominion belongs to the LORD and he rules over the nations. All the rich of the earth will feast and worship; all who go down to the dust will kneel before him—those who cannot keep themselves alive. Posterity will serve him; future generations will be told about the Lord. They will proclaim his righteousness to a people yet unborn: He has done it! (Psalm 22:26-31) *(Note 7)*

Note 1

Mary received a heavenly visitation and she miraculously conceived. Since Mary lived during a time when unwed women who became pregnant were presumed to be adulteresses, according to the law, she could have she could have been stoned to death. "But the angel said to her, "Do not be afraid, Mary; you have found favor with God. You will conceive and give birth to a son, and you are to call him Jesus. He will be great and will be called the Son of the Most High. The Lord will give him the throne of his father David" (Luke 1:30-32). An angel of the Lord also visited Joseph and told him that the child Mary conceived was from the Holy Spirit. I can only imagine the ridicule they both feared. Joseph may have doubted

Mary's truthfulness before he experienced the visitation of the angel. Mary possibly feared for her own life before Joseph took her as his wife, even though she was pledged to marry him. They both believed God and in faith persevered, and the birth of Jesus was a miracle. His death on the cross provided for our salvation, through God's mercy and grace. Jesus died that we might live. He endured the cross; even speaking the very words of Psalm 22:1, because he trusted the Father, and the greatest miracle of all time happened. "Today in the town of David a Savior has been born to you; he is the Messiah, the Lord" (Luke 2:11). "For no word from God will ever fail" (Luke 1:37).

I challenge you to remember these things when you feel forsaken and think that God does not hear your prayer. Always remember that throughout history, as a faithful father, God always came to the defense of his children and they always ended up with the upper hand. Jesus ended up at the right hand of the Father.

"For those God foreknew he also predestined to be conformed to the image of his Son, that he might be the firstborn among many brothers and sisters. And those he predestined, he also called; those he called, he also justified; those he justified, he also glorified" (Romans 8:29-30).

When you answer to the higher calling, have faith that the one who has justified you, God himself, will also vindicate you and bring you to glory. Hold on to this hope when you feel hopeless.

Jesus was not an accident and neither are you; you were predestined just like he was, and created for a purpose. Remember that we are created in the likeness and image of God.

"Then God said, "Let us make mankind in our image, in our likeness, so that they may rule over the fish in the sea and the birds in the sky, over the livestock and all the wild animals, and over all the creatures that move along the ground." (Genesis 1:26).

Jesus described the birth of man as being essential to enter the eternal home he has prepared.

"Jesus answered, "Very truly I tell you, no one can see the kingdom of God unless they are born of water and the Spirit. Flesh gives birth to flesh, but the Spirit gives birth to spirit"" (John 3:5-6). Water refers to physical birth, specifically to the water of the amniotic sac. Water also refers to purification. Purification is related to repentance. So in preparation for the new spiritual life, purification through repentance is a necessity. For we were all born into sin; it was an inherited trait. "Jesus replied, "Very truly I tell you, no one can see the kingdom of God unless they are born again"" (John 3:3). Jesus was referring to being born of the Spirit. It is through the Holy Spirit's assistance that you will be successful. "The Spirit himself testifies with our spirit that we are God's children. Now if we are children, then we are heirs—heirs of God and co-heirs with Christ, if indeed we share in his sufferings in order that we may also share in his glory" (Romans 8:16-17).

Note 2

The psalmist was enduring deep distress; he describes his inner sense of powerlessness under fierce attacks. Bulls and lions are metaphors he uses to describe his enemies. Bashan was noted for lush pastures; therefore its animals were well fed and large, making them strong. People who plan to attack or do attack using slander, deception, or whatever other approach, have the physical tenacity along with the vigor to do so—they seem have the upper hand. They seem to flourish richly in their attack. However, they have not arrived at their final fate if they do not repent. They are used, to accomplish a task at which we are seemingly defeated, but if we persevere as Jesus, Joseph, Mary, and the psalmist did, we too will see miraculous results.

Paul said: "That is why for Christ's sake, I delight in weaknesses, in insults, in hardships, in persecutions, in difficulties. For when I am weak, then I am strong" (2 Corinthians 12:10). "On the contrary, we speak as those approved by God to be entrusted with the gospel. We are not trying to please people but God, who tests our hearts" (1 Thessalonians 2:4).

Envy causes people to do the unimaginable, as was the case during the persecution of Christ. As a Christian, you have within you the Spirit of Christ, and sometimes that's all it takes to be attacked by envious people who do not even understand what spirit they are of, or by which they are being led. I can make this application from personal experience. People have slandered me, mocked me, tried to destroy me (or to at least tried to get me out of their way), to get what I wore (they attempted to defrock me of my position) because they wanted what I had. In essence, they were attacking me the same way Jesus was attacked. From the beginning of his existence, Satan has been trying to take God's position. He seeks to rob steal and destroy and would especially like to remove us from our position in Christ. Therefore we need to be cautious of these attacks, knowing the spiritual motive behind them and react appropriately and not in retaliation. When people attack us we should consider the source and be courageous. "Finally, be strong in the Lord and in his mighty power. Put on the full armor of God, so that you can take your stand against the devil's schemes" (Ephesians 6:10-11).

Due to the increase of wickedness in the world, we must guard our hearts and not allow our love to grow cold or give up on people. Just as Jesus prayed for God to forgive them because they did not know what they were doing, we too must forgive those who sin against us because they are blinded by that sin. What counts is that we allow God to complete the work he started in us, just as Jesus allowed God to complete the work in his life. After all the suffering and distress he went through, he said, *"It is finished."*

"The wind blows wherever it pleases. You hear its sound, but you cannot tell where it comes from or where it is going. So it is with every one born of the Spirit" (John 3:8). The Holy Spirit is sovereign. He works as he pleases in renewing human hearts. "In the same way, the Spirit helps us in our weakness. We do not know what we ought to pray for, but the Spirit himself intercedes for us through wordless groans" (Romans 8:26).

Note 3

Jesus said, "If you believe, you will receive whatever you ask for in prayer" (Matthew 21:22). So keep it in mind that God will never leave you or forsake you. "For the LORD will not reject his people; he will not forsake his inheritance" (Psalm 94:14). "Be strong and courageous. Do not be afraid or terrified because of them, for the LORD your God goes with you; he will never leave you nor forsake you" (Deuteronomy 31:6).

"Whoever gives heed to instruction prospers, and blessed is the one who trusts in the LORD" (Proverbs 16:20). "The greedy stir up conflict, but those who trust in the LORD will prosper" (Proverbs 28:25). "Endure hardship as discipline; God is treating you as his children. For what children are not disciplined by their father?" (Hebrews 12:7). "What, then, shall we say in response these things? If God is for us, who can be against us?" (Romans 8:31). "Who shall separate us from the love of Christ? Shall trouble or hardship or persecution or famine or nakedness or danger or sword?" (Romans 8:35). "No, in all these things we are more than conquerors through him who loved us" (Romans 8:37). "And we know that in all things God works for the good of those who love him, who have been called according to his purpose" (Romans 8:28).

Note 4

Jesus taught us how to pray, and part of that prayer was *"deliver us from evil,"* so we pray, knowing that God hears and will answer. "From the LORD comes deliverance. May your blessings be on your people" (Psalm 3:8). When deliverance comes, it becomes part of our testimony. Our testimony is key in overcoming Satan. In chapter 12 of the book of revelation, he is referred to as the ancient serpent, a dragon that was hurled to earth and the accuser of the brothers and sisters of Christ. "They triumphed over him by the blood of the Lamb and by the word of their testimony; they did not love their lives so much as to shrink from death" (Revelation 12:11).

Note 5
As we appeal to God and trust in his mercy and righteousness, we also acknowledge that he alone delivers us, and we will become testimonies of his goodness and patience with us. As we speak forth the joy God gave us due to relief from our distress, and how we have grown from it, God receives the glory due him in praise.

Note 6
God does not take pleasure in evil. The wicked cannot dwell with him. The arrogant cannot stand in his presence. He hates all who do wrong. He destroys those who tell lies. He abhors bloodthirsty, deceitful men. By his great mercy I will come into his house. In reverence I will bow down toward his holy temple. (All of this was a paraphrase of Psalm 5:4-7.) "Lead me, LORD, in your righteousness because of my enemies—make straight your way before me" (Psalm 5:8). "But you, LORD, are a shield around me, my glory the One who lifts my head high. I call out to the LORD, and he answers me from his holy mountain" (Psalm 3:3-4). "Arise, LORD! Deliver me, my God!" (Psalm 3:7).

Note 7
The eternal life of your heart is based on the internal contents of it. In the Beatitudes, Jesus exemplified the issues of blessing that seem contrary to blessings from a worldly viewpoint. True wealth is richness of heart. We are part of the generation that was often spoken of in Old Testament prophecy. It was prophesied that you would remember and turn to the Lord. Jesus said, "But the Advocate, the Holy Spirit, whom the Father will send in my name, will teach you all things and will remind you of everything I have said to you" (John 14:26). "When the Advocate comes, whom I will send to you from the Father – the Spirit of truth who goes out from the Father – he will testify about me. And you also must testify, for you have been with

me from the beginning" (John 15:26-27). The Holy Spirit helps us to call to mind the words of Christ and the scriptures as we need the application of them in our lives and in fulfillment of our calling as disciples. We have inherited great riches. "Come, all you who are thirsty, come to the waters; and you who have no money, come, buy and eat! Come, buy wine and milk without money and without cost" (Isaiah 55:1). Consider that the wine is symbolic of the Holy Spirit and the milk is the Word of God and it is all free because of what Jesus Christ did for us! You can feast and worship knowing that you are blessed.

> "Blessed are the poor in spirit, for theirs is the kingdom of heaven.
>
> Blessed are those who mourn, for they will be comforted.
>
> Blessed are the meek, for they will inherit the earth.
>
> Blessed are those who hunger and thirst for righteousness, for they will be filled.
>
> Blessed are the merciful, for they will be shown mercy.
>
> Blessed are the pure in heart, for they will see God.
>
> Blessed are the peacemakers, for they will be called children of God.
>
> Blessed are those who are persecuted because of righteousness, for theirs is the kingdom of heaven.
>
> Blessed are you when people insult you, persecute you and falsely say all kinds of evil against you because of me.
>
> Rejoice and be glad, because great is your reward in heaven, for in the same way they persecuted the prophets who were before you." (Matthew 5:3-12)

The Sermon on the Mount could be considered Jesus' inaugural address as King. It explains what he expects of members of his kingdom. The Beatitudes deal with heart issues. To be *blessed* means more than *happiness*, which is an emotion expressed due to outward circumstances. Blessing, as referred to in the beatitudes, is an attitude of spiritual contentment, happiness, and joy, regardless of circumstances. I find it interesting that the actual word *attitude* lies within the word *Beatitudes*. The moral and ethical standard called for in this sermon cannot be achieved in our own power. *Blessed*, as used in the Beatitudes, refers to the ultimate well-being and spiritual joy that is distinctive of those who share in the kingdom of God. The lives of God's children are a stark contrast to the spiritually proud and self-sufficient. The type of blessing that Jesus referred to is a gift of God and not earned. This blessing is imparted to those who give heed to the discipline of God and apply the Word of God to their everyday life, and every trial and situation they face.

> "Look, I am coming soon! My reward is with me, and I will give to each person according to what they have done. I am the Alpha and the Omega, the First and the Last, the Beginning and the End. "Blessed are those who wash their robes, that they may have the right to the tree of life and may go through the gates into the city. Outside are the dogs, those who practice magic arts, the sexually immoral, the murders, the idolaters and everyone who loves and practices falsehood. "I Jesus have sent my angel to give you this testimony for the churches. I am the Root and the Offspring of David, and the bright Morning Star" (Revelation 22:12-16).

> "Those whom I love I rebuke and discipline. So be earnest, and repent. Here I am! I stand at the door and knock. If anyone hears my voice and opens the door, I will come in and eat with that person, and they with me." (Revelation 3:19-20)

This, my friends, might be your last call.

ABOUT THE AUTHOR

Kathleen was born on the military base Camp Lejeune, in North Carolina. She was raised in a suburb of Cleveland, Ohio, by her mother and father who were devout Catholics. She started her quest for deeper knowledge of God after reading a book that inspired her to read the Bible for herself. One day, she met a man who was walking alongside a country road near her home. It was an unforgettable meeting. He had eyes like blue crystals and his long hair and beard were white. He wore a jacket with no buttons, fastened with ties. Thinking he was a transient in need of help, she offered him her lunch, and then attempted to greet him, reaching out to shake his hand. He backed away from her reach and said: "I need nothing from you, but pray to God for an advocate, and pray the Bible with pencil and metal." Many years went by, and while praying, she had a vision of a blank piece of paper with a pencil on it, and saw what she would describe as illuminated particles falling all around her. She heard the title of this book, *Last Call*, and began to write it.

www.ingramcontent.com/pod-product-compliance
Lightning Source LLC
Chambersburg PA
CBHW030327080526
44584CB00012B/739